Foreword

AFTER WRITING OVER 25 books on bridge that discuss certain aspects of play, defense, system, or general bidding, I've begun a series of books aimed at turning aspiring players into good players. Note I don't say expert players. That will be the next step.

Bridge isn't a game where you can immerse yourself for six months and become a good player. There's just too much to learn. You have to start somewhere and then move in the right direction.

Typically, when you start playing in a club, you feel lost. After you get your feet on the ground, you still recognize that you aren't moving very fast. Going forward requires that you get good guidance. Many players at your club will offer advice.

Much of that advice, unfortunately, isn't very good.

This series of books includes hundreds of mini-lessons, complete with insights and advice you can count on. The material is devoted to situations and problems you will see at the table but not in other books.

This book (#2 in a series) won't make you an expert.

But these books will start you on the path to being a good player and a good partner.

Enjoy the trip.

Mike Lawrence

INSIGHTS ON
Bridge

BIDDING, PLAY AND DEFENSE

BOOK 2

MIKE LAWRENCE

BARON
BARCLAY
BRIDGE SUPPLY

PUBLISHED BY:

Baron Barclay Bridge Supplies
3600 Chamberlain Lane, Suite 206
Louisville, KY 40242
U.S. & Canada 1-800-274-2221
Worldwide 502-426-0410
Fax 502-426-2044
www.baronbarclay.com

ISBN: 978-1-944201-33-3

Cover design by Mary Maier
Text design and composition by John Reinhardt Book Design

Printed in the United States of America

South Deals + North-South Vulnerable

WEST	EAST
♠ J 10 8 2	♠ Q 6
♥ 10 3	♥ Q 9 6
♦ A Q 6	♦ J 10 3
♣ 10 9 4 2	♣ K Q J 6 3

WEST	NORTH	EAST	SOUTH
			1♥
Pass	2♥	Pass	Pass
Dbl	Pass	3♣	All pass

BRIDGE IS A funny game. You read books telling you to be cautious about bidding in competition and here comes a crummy hand walking headfirst into the opponents' auction. North and South have the bidding to themselves up to 2♥. To this point, East and West have had no opportunity to do anything. When 2♥ is passed to West, he has to decide whether to pass it out or to reopen.

West's double is based on the principle that you try not to let the opponents play the hand in a low-level contract that they like. When they raise hearts, they have a fit, which is the strongest sign that they are in a good contract. West, with good distribution and not much else, doubles for takeout.

West can infer from the bidding that East has 10–12 points (he might have more) and the ones East has fit this range. They aren't good points but they are enough. Those major-suit queens aren't worth much, plus, East wasn't able to bid spades. Still, 3♣ rates to go down one, which is a good result. If the opponents bid to 3♥, that will be better yet because it may go down.

North Deals + North-South Vulnerable

	WEST		EAST
♠	K 5	♠	J 7
♥	K Q J 6 3 2	♥	9 7
♦	J 2	♦	A K 8 7 4
♣	Q 8 6	♣	K 7 5 3

WEST	NORTH	EAST	SOUTH
	Pass	Pass	Pass
?			

WEST IS IN fourth seat following three passes. What should West's plan be here?

WEST	NORTH	EAST	SOUTH
	Pass	Pass	Pass
2♥	All pass		

WEST'S 2♥ BID looks odd but it is a good bid. In fourth seat, you have the option of passing the hand out. Essentially, in fourth seat, you open if you think you can get a plus score and you pass if you think you will get a minus score.

West's 2♥ bid is therefore constructive. It says you have a full opening bid with a six-card suit but you don't really want to get higher unless partner has a fit with shape and good high-card structure.

Take this hand. 2♥ turns out to buy the hand. North-South might have been able to get in over 1♥ but it was more danger-ous to come in over 2♥, especially when it was known that West has an opening bid.

In addition, the 2♥ bid kept East from getting excited. He passed it out and that ended the bidding. It turns out that even 2♥ is in slight danger and 3♥ is definitely too high.

POSTMORTEM

The guideline for a fourth-seat weak two-bid is that you have an opening bid with a good six-card suit but you have no appealing features to speak of. This means you are usually as balanced as possible, 6-3-2-2, and you have poorish high-card points.

If you agree on this with your partner, I suggest you play that 2NT is your only forcing bid. It promises a fit with useful points. The bidding continues along normal weak two bidding with the one change being that opener's range is about twelve to fourteen instead of six to ten.

QUICKIE

Partner is on your side. If he isn't, why did he agree to play bridge with you? Be as nice to your partner as you expect partner to be to you. When you revoke, do you do it on purpose? Do you think partner is different?

			HAND 3

	WEST	EAST
♠	3 2	♠ K 9 7 6 5
♥	Q	♥ K J 8 7
♦	K Q J 6 3	♦ 2
♣	Q 10 7 5 3	♣ K 6 4

WEST	NORTH	EAST	SOUTH
			1♠
2NT	Pass	3♣	Pass
Pass	Dbl	All pass	

THE PLAY IN 3♣, doubled, was ugly. South led a heart, taken by North's ace. Back came the inevitable singleton spade. South took two spades and continued the suit. From this point on, the play went further downhill for East and the result was down three. Minus 500.

"That's a good result," claimed West. "They are cold for 4♥!"

"Oh?" mulled East.

So West was a little weak on his estimate. 4♥ turns out to be down at least one and more likely, two.

How do you divide the blame for this disaster?

What percentage goes to bad judgment?

What percentage goes to bad luck?

Mostly, the blame goes to West for bad judgment. It was poor. 2NT, even when not vulnerable, should promise some values. Your partner will have to bid at the three level so you need something better than the hand West actually has. The ♥Q is a warning. West would much prefer to have the ♣J instead of the ♥Q.

	WEST		EAST
♠	3 2	♠	K 9 7 6 5
♥	6	♥	K J 8 7
♦	K Q J 6 3	♦	2
♣	Q J 10 7 5	♣	K 6 4

This would be the new layout. Not only would the ♣J be worth a trick, it lessens the chances that 3♣ would be doubled. As it is, this hand is still a minimum 2NT bid when not vulnerable.

Something to think about: When you bid 2NT, there is a decent chance that your partner won't have a three- or four-card suit to bid. He may have only a two-card minor. How do you spell catastrophe?

POSTMORTEM

As always, there was some bad luck. The bad luck was that North was able to double 3♣. Sometimes you will get away with bad bids. Better, though, is not to make bad bids.

Note that East has a pretty good hand. Opposite many 2NT bids, East will make 3♣.

QUICKIE

Learn from the mistakes made at your table. Don't blame them on partner. Sometimes a bad board occurs when both you and your partner contribute to it. Discuss your bad boards. It's more rewarding than talking about your good boards.

West Deals + North-South Vulnerable

EAST

♠ K 5 4
♥ J 7 5 3
♦ K 8 2
♣ A J 7

WEST	NORTH	EAST	SOUTH
1NT	Pass	?	

WEST OPENS A strong notrump. What should East bid?

Many players have concluded that with balanced hands, you shouldn't bother looking for a major. No one hand is proof of this but in the long run, you should find that raising to 3NT is best.

WEST	NORTH	EAST	SOUTH
1NT	Pass	3NT	All pass

The obvious reason is that even if you have a four-four major-suit fit, it may play better in notrump. With no ruffing value, notrump could be best.

The less obvious reason is that this sequence gives away no information.

If you use Stayman and do not find a fit, the opponents will learn a lot about your distributions. For instance, if you bid Stayman and your partner bids spades and you bid 3NT, the defenders know opener has spades and responder has hearts.

This is a lot of information to be handing out.

Further, if you bid 2♣, the opponents sometimes can double for a club lead or at the least, the opening leader will have the gentle inference that his partner did not double for a club lead.

Here's the layout:

	WEST		EAST
♠	A Q 3	♠	K 5 4
♥	Q 8 6 4	♥	J 7 5 3
♦	A Q 7	♦	K 8 2
♣	Q 10 4	♣	A J 7

If you bid 3NT, the defense might lead a heart, the friendliest of leads for your side.

POSTMORTEM

For the record, 4♥ is not cold. It has the potential to lose three (or four) trump tricks and the ♣K. We have all gone down in games like 4♥.

East Deals   +   No One Vulnerable

WEST	EAST
♠ A K Q J 6 5	♠ 10 2
♥ 7 3	♥ K 6 4 2
♦ 5 2	♦ A K Q J 9
♣ A K J	♣ 7 6

THIS HAND IS a reminder that not all older conventions should go away. This hand shows an old-fashioned bid being used.

WEST	NORTH	EAST	SOUTH
		1♦	Pass
2♠	Pass	3♦	Pass
3♠	Pass	4♠	Pass
5♣	Pass	5♦	Pass
5♠	Pass	5NT	Pass
6NT	All pass		

Each opens 1♦ and West jump shifts to 2♠. This is the strong jump shift. Rarely found today. West is announcing a big hand with excellent spades.

So far, so good. East should try to make a descriptive bid when West jump shifts. If he can raise spades, he should do so. If he can bid notrump, he should do so.

East can't do either of these things but he does have a good diamond suit worth rebidding. West rebids his spades, showing a very good suit. Note that the jump shift has committed the hand to game so West doesn't have to do any unnecessary jumping. If West bids anything but 3♠ now, he is guilty of being either foolish or overly innovative. Simple bidding is often the best bidding, and that certainly applies here.

East has nothing new to add and raises to 4♠, which denies any extra values. It does not promise more than one or two little spades.

West isn't ready to give up on slam but with two possible heart losers he can't bludgeon the hand to slam. 5♣ is a cuebid, which will help determine if five is the limit or if seven is possible. East cuebids the ♦A and the problem is back in West's hands.

Can West bid a slam now? No. All West can do is sign off in 5♠. East, fortunately, is still there. East knows that West is looking for a slam and that hearts is the suit West is afraid of. Since East has the ♥K and five likely diamond tricks, East bids 5NT, which shows the ♥K. This gives West information that 6NT rates to be a good contract if played from the East side of the table. He continues to 6NT.

POSTMORTEM

Sadly, strong jump shifts don't seem to have a home today. If you and your partner bid this hand today and don't have the strong jump shift to help, how would you reach 6NT from the East seat?

Give this hand to your friends and see how they do. If they get to 6NT from the East side of the table, sign them up as teammates.

North Deals + East-West Vulnerable

WEST	EAST
♠ 4	♠ J 8 7 3
♥ K 10 6 3	♥ Q 9 8 7 4
♦ A Q 7 4	♦ K J 5
♣ Q J 8 2	♣ A

WEST	NORTH	EAST	SOUTH
	1♠	Pass	Pass
Dbl	Pass	3♥	Pass
4♥	All pass		

TAKEOUT DOUBLES, IN spite of being the most popular convention in the world, present special little problems to catch the unwary. On this sequence, North opened 1♠ and East correctly passed. East is a point away from an opening bid but with a terrible suit, he shows discretion.

West has an easy bid. With an opening bid of his own and with perfect takeout double shape, West reopens with a double.

How many hearts should East bid?

2♥ is out of the question. In support of hearts, East has around thirteen points. He also has five hearts, a terrific value.

In response to a takeout double, you would normally commit to game with this good a hand. But, since West's double was a reopening double, East contents himself with a jump to 3♥.

West now thinks along these lines: "My double was a reopening double so I don't have to have the same strength as if my double was made over the bidder. My partner knows that so his jump should show a little extra."

With this in mind, West can go to 4♥ because he has four points more than his balancing double promised.

Remember that when you double or when your partner doubles, the promised values can vary. A balancing double, for instance, does not promise as much as a double immediately over the opening bidder.

QUICKIE

Can you open 1NT with a five-card major suit?

Experience is showing that it is more than a nice idea. One hidden advantage is that the opponents won't know you have a five-card major. Occasionally, they may lead it to your benefit.

There is another big consideration. If you open 1♥ with sixteen balanced points, you may be embarrassed by a 1♠ response. For this reason, you may feel more inclined to bid 1NT with five hearts than with five spades. For example:

> ♠ J 3
> ♥ A Q 9 8 7
> ♦ K Q 7
> ♣ K J 3

If you open 1♥ and partner bids 1♠, your next bid is difficult.

North Deals + No One Vulnerable

WEST

♠ Q 5
♥ K Q
♦ K 10 4
♣ K Q 7 6 4 3

WEST	NORTH	EAST	SOUTH
	1♠	Pass	2♦
?			

THERE ARE TIMES when an overcall is relatively safe. There are times when an overcall is dangerous. The hand here discusses a dangerous moment.

Should West bid 3♣?

West should not bid. The reasoning is easy. Most two-over-one auctions in America show good hands. If you are playing against a Two Over One system, South's 2♦ bid promises game points.

You have fifteen high-card points. Their bidding suggests they have twenty-four or more. This means that East has one. Well, perhaps two. But he could have none. Here's a rule you need to learn and respect when playing against most American systems.

RULE: If your opponents start with a two-over-one bid, you should not bother bidding.

Here's an example of the kind of dummy you will find.

WEST		EAST	
♠ Q 5		♠ 8 7 6 2	
♥ K Q		♥ J 8 7 5	
♦ K 10 4		♦ 8 6 2	
♣ K Q 7 6 4 3		♣ 8 2	

West either passes 2♦ or he bids 3♣. 3♣ would be down three tricks against friendly defense and it might be down five if things don't go well. You will often get doubled and it will be expensive. It would be wise if West refrained from bidding. Would you?

There are exceptions to this rule.

It's OK to bid if you have the right kind of hand. Assume no one is vulnerable.

♠ A 6 4
♥ K Q J 10 8
♦ 3
♣ 8 7 6 3

It is OK to bid over 2♦ when you have tricks. In this case you don't hurt their bidding but you do indicate a lead for partner.

♠ 3
♥ A Q J 9 8 7 4
♦ 9 7 6 4
♣ 9

It's OK to bid 3♥ to hinder their bidding. You have tricks and you can hope that partner has a little something. It's possible given you have only seven high-card points.

♠ 8 7
♥ Q 6 4
♦ 3
♣ K Q J 8 6 5 3

It's OK to bid 3♣ when you have tricks. Only if partner has nothing for you will you be down 500.

Professional hint:

♠ 4 3
♥ Q 7
♦ 3
♣ K Q J 10 7 6 4 3

You could bid 4♣ with this hand. The opponents won't like that at all.

♠ K J 4
♥ Q 10 8 7 4
♦ Q 8
♣ A Q 5

A final reminder hand. Bidding after your LHO opens 1♠ and your RHO bids 2♦ is insane. Count your likely tricks.

None in spades.
Two in hearts if you are lucky.
None in diamonds.
One in clubs. Maybe two.

If they double you, it's a disaster.
If they don't double you, your 2♥ bid will have gained nothing. Bad odds.

West Deals + No One Vulnerable

	WEST		EAST	
♠	K J 7 3	♠	A 8 2	
♥	J 4	♥	K Q 7	
♦	A K J 4	♦	Q 7 3	
♣	Q 8 3	♣	A 9 7 6	

WEST	NORTH	EAST	SOUTH
1NT	Pass	3NT	All pass

IF YOU BID this hand any other way, you bid too much. The main trap of this hand is that East doesn't get carried away with his fifteen-count. It's a pleasant fifteen-point hand but it lacks tens and nines and its four-card suit isn't very good. West has a maximum of seventeen, which gives East-West a maximum of 32 high-card points. East should raise to 3NT and get it over with.

Note that 3NT is cold and 4NT is in small jeopardy. 6NT has a 1% chance of making. I like better odds than that for my slams.

POSTMORTEM

With 4-3-3-3 hands, the best thing to do is keep it simple. Raise to whatever level of notrump is appropriate. This hand has fifteen points but poor spot cards. 4NT is a serious overbid. Some actually bid more than 4NT. Some use science. Stayman gives away information. Gerber is foolish. This bid tells you how many aces your side has but it doesn't tell you if your partner has a minimum fifteen-count or a seventeen-count. Balanced hands, more than any other, can count on the 33-point standard for 6NT. You may miss a magic slam but you will stay out of trouble on all the other hands.

South Deals + East-West Vulnerable

	WEST		EAST
♠	Q 10 8 5	♠	J 7 6 3 2
♥	8	♥	Q 7 6 4
♦	A J 7 5	♦	Q 6
♣	A K 10 4	♣	8 3

WEST	NORTH	EAST	SOUTH
			1♣
Pass	1♥	Pass	2♥
Dbl	Pass	2♠	All pass

THIS IS AN example of a delayed takeout double. If you read extensively about doubles, this hand will be familiar to you.

South opens 1♣, catching West with a good but unbiddable hand. It will happen. You can have up to eighteen points and not have a good bid over an opponent's opening bid. West has one of these good hands so has to pass. East can't bid over 1♥ but when South raises to 2♥, West is able to enter the auction with a double. This is a takeout double. West couldn't bid the first time but he is still entitled to make a takeout double when a new suit is bid. West is saying he has the unbid suits and there is a strong inference that he has some strength and length in opener's original suit.

POSTMORTEM

Note that West has to have a good hand for this double. West is not balancing. He is entering an ongoing auction against opponents who have unknown strength. For all West knows, North has a good hand.

East has nothing much, but he does have a five-card spade suit. Under the circumstances, East has a pretty good hand. With experience, you will learn to appreciate how good some little hands can be. For instance, the following is a truly bad hand.

♠ 7 6 3	This is an awful hand. I can't think of anything
♥ Q J 7 6	good to say about it.
♦ 6 4 3	
♣ 9 8 3	

♠ J 7 6 3 2	This is the actual East hand. It's not much
♥ Q 7 6 4	to look at but it does have useful values.
♦ Q 6	It has five spades to the jack, a ♦Q that
♣ 8 3	may be useful, and two doubletons.

This hand will teach you to love the little things when you have them.

QUICKIE

Be careful when you arrange your hand. If you overlook an ace, for instance, your auction rates to be awkward regardless of when you discover it.

South Deals   +   Both Sides Vulnerable

	WEST		EAST
♠	K 10 8	♠	9 5 4
♥	A Q 9 8	♥	2
♦	10 9 8 3	♦	J 5
♣	K 7	♣	A Q J 9 8 6 4

WEST	NORTH	EAST	SOUTH
			1♥
Pass	1♠	3♣	Pass
3NT	All pass		

THIS IS A test of your partnership agreements. If West trusts East to have a hand worth a vulnerable 3♣ bid, he should bid 3NT. This will make if North leads a heart (likely) or a spade, and it may make with any other lead.

The key is what West expects East to have for his 3♣ bid. If East is a solid player, bidding 3NT is clear.

Note that 3♣ by East is not entirely safe. However, it qualifies by most standards.

I know some players who wouldn't bid 3♣ with this East hand, but I think this is passive bridge. Winning bridge consists of putting gentle but firm and constant pressure on the opponents.

Note that West doesn't bid 3NT just to show his points and his stoppers. He has stoppers, true, but he also has help in clubs and he has points that will win tricks now. Not later when it is too late. West should pass if he has something like this hand:

♠ K Q J 2
♥ Q J 3
♦ K 9 4 3 2
♣ 7

This hand has points and stoppers, but it has no fast tricks. Even if East has seven running clubs (virtually impossible), this hand doesn't make 3NT if the defense leads hearts. Passing shows good judgment.

East-West have 20 points between them. Normally one expects 3NT to take 25 points. When you have sure tricks and stoppers, you will find that 3NT can be bid and made on sixteen points. Maybe even less.

West Deals + North-South Vulnerable

_____

EAST

♠ 9 3
♥ A 10 9 4
♦ Q 7
♣ A 10 6 5 3

WEST	NORTH	EAST	SOUTH
2♦	2♥	?	

IF YOU OPEN weak two-bids, you can expect to hear lots of competitive bidding. It's good to open lots of weak twos and other preempts, but doing so is only half of the battle. Your partnership has to know how to continue the bidding too.

Here, West opens a routine weak two-bid and North overcalls 2♥. What should East do?

If East could get South to promise to pass 2♥, East might pass and try to beat it. But you know and I know that if East passes, South may be able to bid 2♠. Can East do anything good here?

WEST	NORTH	EAST	SOUTH
2♦	2♥	3♦	?

East's 3♦ bid does two things. It competes for a plus score. After all, 3♦ might make. And it gets in South's way. If South has an eight-point hand with five or six decent spades, he might bid them at the two level. If he has to bid them at the three level, he might decide that's too rich and pass instead.

Here's the East-West layout:

	WEST	EAST
♠	8 4	9 3
♥	6 5	A 10 9 4
♦	A K 9 8 5 3	Q 7
♣	J 9 7	A 10 6 5 3

There are many benefits to be had from aggressive preempting. You may feel that 2♦ is automatic on the West hand, but I promise you that many players will pass it for one reason or another. Because West did open 2♦, East was able to get that 3♦ bid in before the opponents found their spade suit.

It appears that West may make 3♦. It also appears that North-South can make nine or ten tricks in spades. East's 3♦ bid may be enough to stop that from happening.

Of casual note, you should be aware that East's ♣10 is useful to West in a 3♦ contract. Even West's ♣9 plays a constructive role. Spot cards are often the key to success.

HAND 12

EAST

♠ –
♥ K Q 9 7 4 3
♦ A J 7 4
♣ K 10 3

WEST	NORTH	EAST	SOUTH
	1♣	1♥	Pass
2♥	Pass	?	

WHAT SHOULD EAST bid?

East's hand has grown enormously.

He has a sixth heart.
He has a spade void.
He has excellent-quality high cards.

There's nothing about the East hand that isn't to like. He should bid 4♥. It turns out East will make 4♥ with no trouble.

Now, how should East bid if West responds 1♠?

WEST	NORTH	EAST	SOUTH
	1♣	1♥	Pass
1♠	Pass	?	

East would know that 1♠ isn't a good spot and would probably bid 2♥. West would probably pass.

Here's the layout:

WEST	EAST
♠ 10 8 7 5 3 2	♠ –
♥ J 10 8	♥ K Q 9 7 4 3
♦ K 3	♦ A J 7 4
♣ Q 7	♣ K 10 3

The whole point of this hand is what West should do when East overcalls 1♥. I think West should raise hearts. East usually has five and may have six. Yes, I know that four is possible, but that is rare. In any event, how likely is it that East has enough spades that spades will be a better spot than hearts? In my opinion, finding a major-suit fit is a prime objective and the way to do that is to tell partner when you have a fit. Why be greedy and look for another?

Look at this from East's point of view. What bid does East most want to hear when he bids 1♥? He wants to hear a raise. That is the best news East can hear. If West bids 1♠, he may lose the chance to bid 2♥. It's true that East will bid hearts again but the West hand isn't good enough to go further. West has the proper values to bid 2♥ and that gives East information he can use.

I showed this theme in *Insights on Bridge, Book 1*. It comes up often enough that it bears repeating.

If you don't raise immediately, you won't get a second chance to accurately show you really do like partner's suit.

HAND 13

	WEST		EAST
♠	7	♠	A J 8 6 4
♥	A K J 8	♥	10 9 5 3
♦	A J 10 5 3	♦	6 4
♣	9 8 5	♣	K Q

WEST	NORTH	EAST	SOUTH
			1♦
1♥	Pass	?	

SINCE I HAVE mentioned elsewhere that a four-card overcall is possible, I felt it only fair to include one. I am an advocate of four-card overcalls if properly used. This hand meets all the requirements. West has a very good suit, a good hand, can bid at the one level, and has no other way to get into the auction other than with an overcall. (Anyone who makes a takeout double deserves to hear his partner jump in spades.)

POSTMORTEM

I'm not showing the complete auction because there are many ways for East to show a hand worth a limit raise.

The point of this hand is that if partner makes a limit raise, which promises four-card support, West has plenty to go to game.

Here's my suggestion for raising partner's overcall.

WEST	NORTH	EAST	SOUTH
			1♦
1♥	Pass	?	

2♦   A cuebid shows a limit raise or better with three trumps.

2♥   The simple raise shows 6–9 points with three or four trumps. Just the same as when West has opened the bidding. When you have six points with something your partner is sure to like, make the raise. It will help your partner's judgment.

3♦   A jump cuebid shows a limit raise or better with four trumps.

3♥   The jump raise is preemptive. It promises shape plus 4–7 support points. In other words, the hand is good for partner, but does not imply much strength.

Since East-West have a good play for 4♥, it's fair to say that there should be a way to bid it. Here, the bidding goes smoothly as long as West is aware that overcalling at the one level with a four-card suit is a good strategy. The conversation has to start somewhere and 1♥ is really the only way to start that conversation.

HAND 14

	WEST		EAST
♠	8 7 4 3	♠	K Q 2
♥	3 2	♥	A K Q 9 6 4
♦	10 7 6 4	♦	Q 3
♣	8 7 5	♣	A Q

WEST	NORTH	EAST	SOUTH
		2♣	Pass
2♦*	Pass	2♥	Pass
3♣**	Pass	3♥	All pass

* WAITING;
** VERY BAD HAND

HOW FORCING ARE your 2♣ bids? If you rebid 2NT, you are showing a notrump hand. Partner can pass that. But if opener rebids a suit, is it game forcing or are you allowed to stop short of game when responder has a bad hand? The agreement most players use is this one.

The 2♣ bid is forcing until opener bids and rebids a suit. On this hand, opener rebids 2♥. If responder makes the weak bid of 3♣ (or whatever you use for your second negative), and opener bids 3♥, it can be passed.

Note that if opener bids a second suit after the 3♣ bid, it is forcing.

	WEST	EAST
	2♣	2♦
	2♥	3♣
	3♦	

3♦ is forcing. Opener may have a hand so strong that it does not want partner to pass.

Alternatively, if responder does anything other than show weakness, the auction is forcing.

	WEST	EAST
	2♣	2♦
	2♥	2♠
	3♥	

On this sequence, responder bid 2♠, promising something more than a bust. In this case, the bidding is forcing to game without fail.

EAST

♠ J 8 7 6 4 2
♥ 3 2
♦ 4
♣ K 6 5 4

WEST	NORTH	EAST	SOUTH
			1♥
2♣	2♠	?	

PLAYERS TODAY KNOW that it is a good idea to strike before the opponents get their act together.

You have seen that preempting is an effective strategy. Most people think of preempts as being opening bids. This hand shows a different kind of preempt.

East knows that North-South have a game somewhere. It's not impossible that they have a slam. What should East bid?

WEST	NORTH	EAST	SOUTH
			1♥
2♣	2♠	4♣	

This is a good time to preempt. East has four good trumps. He has a singleton. He expects that the opponents have a game and maybe a slam. Instead of passing or bidding 3♣, East should bid at least 4♣, taking away important bidding room.

Is this dangerous? Not really. Assuming that West has a proper vulnerable 2♣ overcall, East can pretty much count on five or six club tricks and a couple of diamond ruffs in dummy. West might have another trick somewhere. West should be able to take eight tricks, and that will be a success. Even if 4♣ is doubled, it will go down only 500. North-South rate to make 620 or more.

If you wish, you might even bid 5♣ in the hope that:

1. The opponents keep bidding.
2. Your partner can take nine tricks.

A preempt like this one is fairly common. But it does require judgment. I can vouch for the effectiveness of these bids. I've been on the receiving end and I've been the one who makes bids like this. They work as long as they are done properly. They are a real annoyance for the opponents to deal with.

If you make a bid like 5♣ on the example hand here, it may be that your side is going to go down 800 for a bad score. Keep in mind that your opponents are not perfect. They may take the bait and bid on themselves. Perhaps they will get to 5♥ going down one trick. Perhaps they'll misjudge and bid to 6♥ and go down. This could happen because the opponents can't ask for aces over your 5♣ bid. Preempts in all guises are formidable. When they work, they are wonderful.

Importantly, in the hand being discussed, both sides are vulnerable. If the opponents are vulnerable and you are not, then 5♣ is surely the right bid.

Here's a possible layout:

```
              ♠ A K 10 9 3
              ♥ Q 8
              ♦ Q 10 9 2
              ♣ 8 7

♠ 5                              ♠ J 8 7 6 4 2
♥ J 9 7                          ♥ 3 2
♦ K 5 3                          ♦ 4
♣ A Q J 9 3 2                    ♣ K 6 5 4

              ♠ Q
              ♥ A K 10 6 5 4
              ♦ A J 8 7 6
              ♣ 10
```

If East bids 4♣, South will have a decision to make. Probably he will bid 4♦. North has to guess to bid 4♥ or 5♦. Whichever bid he chooses, South has to refrain from getting too high.

If East bids 5♣, South has a similarly difficult decision.

If someone doubles 5♣, it only goes down two tricks. If South keeps bidding, he likely will end up in a slam that won't make.

Make your opponents guess.

North Deals   +   North-South Vulnerable

WEST	EAST
♠ A 2	♠ 9 7
♥ 10 9 6 4 2	♥ J 5
♦ K 8 3	♦ A Q J 10 6 2
♣ 10 8 4	♣ A K 7

WEST	NORTH	EAST	SOUTH
	1♠	2♦	2♠
3♦	Pass	3♠	Dbl
3NT	All pass		

ONE OF THE most abused conventions I know of is something called the Western cuebid. I see it on lots of convention cards, but I seldom see it used correctly. On this sequence, East makes a sound 2♦ overcall and West raises to 3♦, as he should. East, if he visualizes his hand correctly, can more or less count on eight tricks. If West has a spade stopper, 3NT will have a chance. This is what East's 3♠ bid does. It asks West if he has a stopper in spades, the opponents' suit. Note that stoppers in other suits are not known to exist. When the bidding gets this high, it is hard to be sure about all the other suits as well as the opponents' suit.

South's double of 3♠ allows West to pass, but with a genuine spade stopper and with a magic ♦K, he is better placed to bid 3NT. That is what East asked for, and West has the answer.

Usually, the Western cuebid is used at the three level. It is most often used after a fit is found and a source of tricks is discovered. Then, the Western cuebid can be used.

South Deals + North-South Vulnerable

WEST

♠ Q 9 8 6 3
♥ K 8 2
♦ A K J 8
♣ 8

WEST	NORTH	EAST	SOUTH
			1♥
1♠	2♥	Pass	Pass
?			

HOW FAR SHOULD one go to compete? Knowing when to compete and when to quit is an art form. Here's what West should be thinking.

The bidding shows that North-South have 19–22 high-card points, so East is marked for a few values. Since East didn't raise spades and since East is marked for only two hearts (the opponents bid and raised them), East will have most of his length in the minor suits. 3♦ is not a bad bid. He can easily have four diamonds. Five is possible. In either case, 3♦ will often be a good contract. And much of the time it won't matter because the opponents will bid to 3♥.

POSTMORTEM

West's spade overcall is impeccable. The suit could be better but the hand strength is fine. You must take some risks when you bid. If you wait for the perfect hand, you will lose on many other hands where an overcall would have been good. Don't worry that the sky is falling every time you open your mouth.

If playing matchpoints, 3♦ is almost mandatory. You have little chance of setting 2♥, which will be an awful result. The odds on something good coming from a 3♦ bid are reasonable.

Much the same goes for playing in a team game. The risk of seeing them make 2♥ is huge. The risk in bidding is minimal.

Here's the East-West layout:

	WEST	EAST	
♠	Q 9 8 6 3	♠ 7 4	
♥	K 8 2	♥ 9 3	
♦	A K J 8	♦ 10 7 6 3	
♣	8	♣ A Q 10 4 2	

WEST	NORTH	EAST	SOUTH
			1♥
1♠	2♥	Pass	Pass
3♦	All pass		

East's hand is actually a little bit of a disappointment. It has four diamonds. It might have had five. It has six high-card points. They are decent points but still, he might have had a little more. The ♦Q, for instance, would be nicer than the ♣Q.

	WEST	EAST
♠	2	Q 10 9 5 4
♥	K 7 2	J 6
♦	A Q J 10 6 5 3	K 9
♣	Q J	A K 7 3

WEST	NORTH	EAST	SOUTH
1♦	2♠*	Pass	Pass
3♦	Pass	3NT	All pass

*Weak

WEST'S 1♦ BID is correct, as is East's pass. East wants West to reopen with a double, which East will pass for penalty (assuming you are using negative doubles). When 2♠ gets back to West, he has to find a good way to reopen the bidding.

It is possible that East has a penalty pass hand so West has to reopen if there is a sensible way to do it. In this case, West can bid 3♦, which is descriptive and sensible.

Note that West does not reopen with a double. West has a poor defensive hand. 3♦ is the only realistic bid West can make. If West tries a double it will work on this hand, but it will fail when East has a lesser hand.

East's 3NT bid is correct. East has to take a small chance on hearts, but it is an acceptable risk. West is a favorite to have a high card in hearts. In any event, there is no safe way for East to work it out.

I noted that West should consider that East may have a spade stack and is hoping for a reopening double. This possibility is one of the things that opener must always think about when the bidding goes as shown. This auction is commonplace. It pays to be alert to the possibility that East has a good hand with the opponent's suit.

West, on this hand, has very minimum defense against a spade contract, even if East wants to defend against 2♠ doubled. What West has is a good hand for diamonds.

QUICKIE

Never add a convention to your methods if you have not agreed on how to play the convention. Saying you will use Jacoby is not sufficient. When you use a convention, you have to know all the parts to it. It's like going to an auto dealer and buying a quart of oil for your ailing car. You better know where to put it. If you put it in the window washer system…

South Deals + North-South Vulnerable

	WEST		EAST
♠	K Q 10 8 6 4	♠	–
♥	6	♥	Q 10 8 4 2
♦	A Q 3	♦	J 8 6 5
♣	Q J 8	♣	K 7 6 5

WEST	NORTH	EAST	SOUTH
			1♠
Pass	1NT*	Pass	2♠
Dbl	All pass		

* FORCING

SOUTH OPENS 1♠, showing five or more spades. What would you do if you were holding the West hand and heard South open 1♠? I'd be tempted to check the backs of the cards, but would pass as smoothly as possible. No need to fret and tell South that his spades are breaking this badly.

North responds 1NT, forcing, and South rebids his spades, showing six. West is delighted. How delighted is he? Given he has lots of spade tricks and some other defense, he can double 2♠ for penalty. East passes and the only question now is how many tricks South will get. Two items of note:

1. West has good spade spots. These often play an important role.
2. West has defense, which will be useful if North runs to another suit.

ASIDE: If South had opened 1♣ or 1♦ and North bid 1NT, and South rebid his minor, a double by West would best be played as some kind of belated takeout double. See the next hand for a discussion on this.

POSTMORTEM

How can East judge that West is making a penalty double?

East knows that South has six or seven spades. North did not raise spades. North has, at most, two spades. West can have as many as seven spades and usually will have five or six. Be sure you see the logic in this double. If West doubles for penalty and East decides it is for takeout, it will be a disaster. That would be sad given that South was about to go down a lot.

If East thinks that West's double is for takeout, he will bid something. If he does choose to bid, 3♥ would be a likely choice. That won't be a winning decision. You can see the East-West layout above. 3♥ will be a horrible contract.

It's important to know partner's intentions when he doubles something.

QUICKIE

Be nice to your partner. You're stuck with each other until the end of the game. (Maybe longer!)

EAST

♠ K Q 7 3
♥ J 8 2
♦ K 2
♣ J 7 6 3

WEST	NORTH	EAST	SOUTH
			1♣
Pass	1NT	Pass	2♣
Dbl	Pass	?	

THIS AUCTION IS a followup to the auction on the previous page. This hand shows a double that is often overlooked or misunderstood. I suggest reading this discussion more than once.

South opens 1♣ and North bids 1NT showing 8–10 high-card points and denying a major. South rebids 2♣.

West doubles. What should East think this double is?

East should consider that the 1NT response includes some clubs and given South is rebidding them, West must have short clubs. West's double is sort of a balancing double. West has already passed so can't have a normal value double.

East should bid 2♠, happy that he has a few values, ending a nice balancing auction. Here's the layout:

WEST	EAST
♠ A 10 8 4	♠ K Q 7 3
♥ Q 7 6 3	♥ J 8 2
♦ Q J 8 4	♦ K 2
♣ 4	♣ J 7 6 3

If West doesn't double 2♣, it will be passed out. 2♣ is sure to make. That will be a very poor result. West has to double and East has to recognize that it is for takeout. Making 2♠ or 3♠ is much better.

POSTMORTEM

Here's a useful set of guidelines.

If opener bids and rebids a suit after his partner responds in a suit at the one level, a double by the next player is penalty.

WEST	NORTH	EAST	SOUTH
			1♦
Pass	1♥	Pass	2♦
Dbl			

WEST	NORTH	EAST	SOUTH
			1♥
Pass	1♠	Pass	2♥
Dbl			

Double is for penalty in both of these cases.

If opener bids a major and rebids it after his partner responds 1NT, a double by the next player is penalty.

WEST	NORTH	EAST	SOUTH
			1♥
Pass	1NT	Pass	2♥
Dbl			

Double is for penalty. This auction was discussed in the previous article.

If South opens either minor and rebids it after his partner responds 1NT, a double by the next player is takeout. This is the situation covered in this discussion.

WEST	NORTH	EAST	SOUTH
			1♦
Pass	1NT	Pass	2♦
Dbl			

Double is for takeout.
Finally, a tricky one.

WEST	NORTH	EAST	SOUTH
			1♦
Pass	1NT	Pass	2♣
Dbl			

This double is also for takeout. It requires an agreement but it is worth it.

These doubles are important. They may not occur that often but when they do, they are big deals. Good to recognize them.

IN THE WORLD of competitive bidding, doubles can be used in many ways. The previous two hands showed an example of a double being used for penalty and another example where a double should be used as takeout. Here's another situation where a double needs to be understood.

WEST	NORTH	EAST	SOUTH
			1♥
Pass	1NT	Pass	2♦
Dbl			

What is West's double all about here? Specifically, is it penalty or is it takeout?

♠ A 10 4 3
♥ 8 7 3
♦ 4 3
♣ A K 10 7

This hand would like to be in the bidding but when South opened 1♥, it was too dangerous to bid.

The answer is to play that when the opponents bid two suits, as they do here, a double by you is for takeout. You are showing a decent hand with spades and clubs. Here's another example in the same vein.

WEST	NORTH	EAST	SOUTH
			1♦
Pass	1♠	Pass	2♠
Dbl			

Again, the opponents have bid two suits. West's double is takeout. What does West have? Here's a typical hand:

♠ 4 3
♥ K 10 7 6
♦ K J 2
♣ A K 10 5

West shows a decent hand with the two unbid suits. You can't bid hearts on the first round and a takeout double with the ♠43 is dangerous. If you agree that you would like to make a bid with this hand, you can use the pass-and-then-double auction shown here.

QUICKIE

When your right hand opponent opens the bidding and you have a good hand, it is not necessary to bid. You can have an eighteen-point hand that is not suitable to bid with. Pass and hope for a second chance. Having points is not always the right reason for bidding.

	WEST	EAST
♠	8 4	♠ J 7 3
♥	K Q 10 7 6 5 3	♥ J 8 2
♦	8 7 2	♦ Q 3
♣	10	♣ K J 8 7 5

WEST	NORTH	EAST	SOUTH
3♥	Pass	4♥	Dbl
Pass	4♠	All pass	

FIRST, REGARDING THE West hand. I have been touting that you should preempt more when you have a good suit and little or nothing on the side. This hand is a trick or so too weak for a 'book' preempt, but at the table, it is automatic as far as I am concerned.

East has two choices. Pass and 4♥.

If East bids 4♥, North-South will lose some bidding room.

If East passes, South will bid something. Say South doubles. North has room to respond 3♠, 4♠, 3NT, or he can even cuebid 4♥. If East raises to 4♥, South can still double but North won't have any room for expression.

POSTMORTEM

If East raises to 4♥ and it gets doubled, West will get six heart tricks and one diamond ruff. That's down 500. A good result given that North-South have a cold 4♠. On this hand, they might even have a slam. East's being a pest damages the North-South bidding.

West Deals + No One Vulnerable

	WEST		EAST
♠	A K 7	♠	8 3
♥	A K 6	♥	9 5
♦	A Q	♦	J 8 6 5
♣	A K J 8 2	♣	Q 9 7 4 3

WEST	NORTH	EAST	SOUTH
2♣	Pass	2♦*	Pass
3♣	Pass	5♣	Pass
6♣	All pass		

*WAITING

NOT A BAD hand. West starts with the big one, 2♣, and gets the expected 2♦ response. West can choose from some number of notrump and 3♣. If West rebids 3NT or 4NT, showing points, East will have no idea how to continue no matter what his hand.

3♣ is a better choice because it keeps more options open. East may have a major suit to show. If he has a miserable hand he can bid 3♦, which, by agreement, shows a bust hand.

If you do not have this agreement, how do you handle hands like this?

♠	6 5 3
♥	9 5 4 2
♦	8 7 6 2
♣	Q 7

East's raise to 5♣ is consistent with the rule that says a jump to game after a strong two-bid shows a poor hand with decent shape and lots of trumps. That is what East has. West has a clear continuation to slam.

West shouldn't bid 7♣. It might make but West can't be sure. Let's say you do bid 7♣ and you make it. Was it necessary to bid seven to get a good score? Since 6NT is a bad contract, just being in 6♣ will get you a good score. There is no need to jeopardize a good score in order to get a little more.

Note that if East had a more useful hand, he would not bid 5♣.

♠ Q 3
♥ 9 5
♦ K J 10 7 4
♣ Q 10 7 4

With this hand he would raise to 4♣. This bid would tell West that East has real values. Reaching a grand slam is likely now.

QUICKIE

Have a positive attitude. Don't spend time thinking why what you are doing is wrong. Instead, think of why it could be right. Believe in yourself.

No one is always right. Not you, not me, not your opponents, and not your partner.

South Deals + East-West Vulnerable

EAST

♠ 9 8 4 3
♥ –
♦ Q 8 7 6
♣ Q 9 7 6 4

WEST	NORTH	EAST	SOUTH
			1♠
2♥	Pass	Pass	Dbl
Pass	Pass	?	

SOUTH OPENED 1♠ and West overcalled 2♥. This was passed to South, who reopened with a double. Things weren't scary until North passed the double for penalty. Now things are officially scary. North's pass says he has hearts and East is prepared to agree with that opinion.

Can East do anything about it?

I would pass 2♥ doubled. One reason is that West should have a good suit for the two-level overcall. Another reason is that saving West requires that you get to the three level.

With the hand East has, he shouldn't bet the farm that his ♣Q9764 is a safe home. This is not the kind of suit you want to escape to. It's made worse by the fact that you would have to go to 3♣.

If East had 5-5 in the minors, a redouble would have slight appeal. But being a level higher in search of a better spot is not clearly worth it.

Here's the unpleasant layout. It looks like West's 2♥ bid got him into trouble. That's one of the risks of bidding. In this case West bid 2♥ on a superb hand and got caught.

	WEST	EAST
♠	K J 7 2	♠ 9 8 4 3
♥	A Q J 9 4 2	♥ –
♦	K 2	♦ Q 8 7 6
♣	8	♣ Q 9 7 6 4

West is in trouble. But the trouble in hearts is less than being doubled at the three level.

There's a humorous slant to this hand. If West can somehow get to a spade contract, he will have a fair chance of escaping. It's rare to escape to opener's suit but it can happen.

West Deals   +   North-South Vulnerable

	WEST		EAST
♠	Q J 8 2	♠	K 10 7 3
♥	K J	♥	Q 7 3
♦	A K J 9 5 2	♦	7 4
♣	3	♣	J 8 6 5

WEST	NORTH	EAST	SOUTH
1♦	Pass	1♠	Pass
?			

THIS HAND OFFERS a bidding trick that is worth looking at. The question on this hand is what West should rebid over 1♠. Here are your choices. Number four may be new to you.

1. You can jump to 3♠.
2. You can jump to 4♠.
3. You can jump to 4♣, showing a singleton with spade support.
4. You can jump to 4♦, showing six diamonds, four spades, and about seventeen support points.

I think the West hand is worth a game bid of some sort. 3♠ isn't forcing and I would hate to hear my partner pass it.

I offer the other choices to show you some of the methods available to opener. If you can raise to game in various ways, you can tell partner the kind of raise you have. This will be necessary whenever responder has a few cards and wants to consider a slam.

I like to play that a jump to game promises a balanced hand. A 4♠ bid shows 19–20 support points and it denies a singleton.

This is a huge help to partner's decision making, knowing that you have a balanced hand. Here's a routine 4♠ bid:

♠   A J 10 9
♥   K Q 7
♦   Q J 9 8
♣   A J

4♣ would be a splinter bid showing 16–20 high-card points with a singleton club. It would look like this:

♠   K Q J 9
♥   A Q 7
♦   A J 10 8 4
♣   J

Finally, when opener jumps to four of his minor, he is showing a shapely hand that is mildly preemptive but is still a strong playing hand. This bid looks like the one West has.

WEST	EAST
♠ Q J 8 2	♠ K 10 7 3
♥ K J	♥ Q 7 3
♦ A K J 9 5 2	♦ 7 4
♣ 3	♣ J 8 6 5

West wishes to raise to game but the value of the hand is not in high-card points but in extreme shape. East as nothing much so will sign off in 4♠, which West will pass. Hopefully, East will make it.

If using the jump to four of opener's minor doesn't appeal to you, don't bother with it.

However, if you play splinters, I endorse them for sure. Then you can play that a jump to four of partner's major promises a balanced hand. In either case, your partner will learn a lot about your hand and that will help his bidding judgment.

QUICKIE

You open 1NT holding two four-card majors. Partner bids 2♣, asking for a major suit. Which major do you bid?

There's not a lot of difference which one you bid but for the sake of consistency, you and your partner should agree which one you will bid when holding both. I suggest that you bid hearts first. The reason is that partner can bid 2♠ over 2♥ if he wishes. Rebidding 2♠ takes up a little more bidding room.

WEST	EAST
♠ 6	♠ K 9 7 4
♥ K J 10 9 6 3	♥ 8
♦ A K 8 3	♦ Q 9 5 4
♣ J 3	♣ K 8 7 5

WEST	NORTH	EAST	SOUTH
	1♣	Pass	1♥
2♥	All pass		

THIS IS A case where a cuebid of an opponent's suit should be natural. West has a fine heart suit plus a good hand as well. Since South is expected to respond in a four-card major, it could be four small ones.

There are two reasons for bidding 2♥. Firstly, the hand is good enough that as long as a 2♥ bid is understood to be natural, the hand is worth bidding with. Secondly, almost no opponent will know what to do when you bid 2♥.

Note, as an aside, that North-South have a 4-4 spade fit. If West passes 1♥, North will rebid 1♠ and South will raise. If West did pass over 1♥, he will have to bid them at the three level or not at all. Better to bid 2♥, which does two things. It shows your hand plus it makes life hard on the opponents.

This is an effective bidding tool if used properly. But it won't work at all if your partner misunderstands your bid.

North Deals   +   East-West Vulnerable

	WEST		EAST
♠	8 3	♠	9
♥	A 10 8 7 2	♥	K Q 9 5
♦	K 10 7 2	♦	Q 9 3
♣	Q 8	♣	A J 7 6 2

WEST	NORTH	EAST	SOUTH
	1♠	Dbl	2♠
4♥	4♠	Pass	Pass
Dbl	All pass		

WHEN BOTH SIDES have a fit, there is often bidding galore. This happens because both sides have shape and distributional points, which means the total number of points in the deck is closer to 50 than 40.

On this hand, there's lots of bidding. East makes a normal takeout double and West jumps to game based on his working points and his fifth heart. 3♥ would be just a little bit conservative. Here comes North with his 4♠ bid.

East, who has his original bid, has nothing more to say. West has nothing extra but he knows that his bid was based on both high cards and distribution. West has good defense for his bid and shows it by doubling. The result will depend on North-South's distribution so the final result is unclear. Down three is possible. Making is also possible. The usual result should be down two.

POSTMORTEM

Doubles like this one don't have to succeed. However, the odds are with you. The key to this double is that your side has half or more of the high-card points and the opponents are under pressure in the bidding. It's not uncommon for North to bid 4♠, as he does here, when he has no expectation of making it. He may be hoping to go down one or two. Best for him would be to go down one or two undoubled. Best for you would be to double them. See the next hand for another example of this double.

QUICKIE

When you have perfect shape for a takeout double, you can be more aggressive than most textbooks suggest. For instance:

WEST	NORTH	EAST	SOUTH
		1♦	?

♠ A J 9 3
♥ K 10 8 3
♦ 3
♣ Q 10 9 3

This is only ten high-card points. But the shape is perfect. No matter what suit partner bids, you have four-card support. True, partner may bid notrump, which you won't like, but the potential gain is worth it. If your partner can bid a suit you are in excellent shape. Note that this hand has good spot cards.

WEST	EAST
♠ 7 4	♠ 8 5
♥ A Q 9 7 3	♥ K 10 6 2
♦ K J 4 3	♦ Q 7 6
♣ K 2	♣ A 10 7 3

WEST	NORTH	EAST	SOUTH
1♥	3♠	4♥	4♠
Pass	Pass	Dbl	All pass

THIS IS AN example of not allowing yourself to be pushed around.

You have seen this theme frequently at the table. It showed up in the previous hand.

Stealing is one of the goals of every bridge player in the world. Swiping a hand from the opponents is much more satisfying than earning it.

East has a hand that would like to make a limit raise. North's 3♠ bid forced East to the four level or to pass, and East made the correct overbid of 4♥. South continued to 4♠ and West passed, as he should. West has a minimum opening bid with nothing special to offer.

When it gets back to East, East has a choice. He can pass, having overbid a little already. He can bid 5♥, overbidding again. Or he can make a general-purpose double of 4♠. One of the hardest things for new players to recognize is that opponents aren't perfect. They bid too much. They don't always overbid, but there are occasions when they not only overbid, they do so on purpose. That's what is probably happening here.

East doesn't know that North-South will go down in 4♠, but he is entitled to take that view. East has nine high-card points and West opened the bidding. East-West rate to have 22 or more high-card points, and that suggests North-South are too high. In general, that in itself is enough to double 4♠. You will learn when to double as you see certain kinds of auctions unfold. This auction, where one opponent made a weak preempt, is a common sequence where you double them on principle.

Note that a preemptive bid by the opponents is not automatically a reason to double them when they stop bidding. Double only when your side has most of the points and you think your side has gotten to its limit.

POSTMORTEM

You can see that East has four hearts. He should not feel that there are no heart winners for East-West against a spade contract. There is usually one and sometimes two. Don't take a negative view just because you fear someone has a void.

If you start making these doubles and if you are successful, you will get recognized as someone not to be messed with.

HAND 29	WEST	EAST

	WEST	EAST
♠	10 8 4 3	♠ A 6
♥	A 8	♥ K Q 10 7 6 4
♦	A 5 3	♦ Q 9
♣	K Q J 3	♣ 10 8 4

WEST	NORTH	EAST	SOUTH
1♣	Pass	1♥	Pass
1♠	Pass	3♥	Pass
4♥	All pass		

WEST OPENS 1♣ and East responds 1♥. So far, so good. What should West rebid? I believe that West should bid 1♠. The idea is that this is the last time for opener to show his four-card spade suit. If East doesn't have spades, nothing has been lost. Now, assuming West rebids 1♠, we get to the real problem of this hand. What should East rebid after 1♠?

The answer depends on your methods. Do you know for sure what a 3♥ bid shows now? Is it forcing? Is it invitational? Does it show five hearts or does it promise six or more?

Sooner or later, you will discover that the majority of players play second round jumps by responder as invitational. If that is your understanding, East can bid 3♥. This shows 11–12 support points for hearts with a good six-card suit. On this hand, West will continue to 4♥ since he has a little more than a minimum and he has a mild heart fit too. If West has a minimum hand, he may pass. West would pass 3♥ with this hand:

♠ K Q J 7
♥ 3
♦ Q 9 8
♣ K J 7 6 4

However, what West does isn't the important issue.

What is important is that your partnership knows for sure what that 3♥ bid means. Either you define it as invitational or you define it as forcing.

There have been many occasions at the table when I asked an opponent if their partner's last bid was forcing or invitational. I get answers ranging from a precise "It's invitational" to something like "I think it is invitational. But I'm not sure. I mean, uh, I mean it's almost forcing. Um. I'm going to bid. No, wait! We play fourth suit forcing so…"

You get the point. A partnership that doesn't know when a bid is forcing is in trouble.

POSTMORTEM

In the discussion, I focused on one specific auction. There are other auctions which require definition.

1♣	1♥
1♠	3♣
1♣	1♥
1♠	3♠
1♣	1♥
1♠	2NT

This is a short list of jumps where the definition of the jump can be invitational or forcing. Your partnership needs to know the answers.

My suggestion is that you should play these jumps as invitational. The reason is that most players play them that way, which means you will have more players to play with and fewer misunderstandings along the way.

QUICKIE

When the bidding by your side goes:

NORTH	SOUTH
1NT	2♣
2♦	2♥

do you and your partner know what you are showing? Is 2♥ forcing, invitational, or a signoff? All treatments are reasonable, but it is important to have some agreement. You can't bid 2♥ or 2♠ and expect partner to know what you have if you don't discuss it in advance.

HAND
30

	WEST	EAST
♠	K Q J 10	♠ A 9 6 2
♥	3	♥ A J
♦	A K J 10 7 6	♦ Q 4
♣	A 3	♣ Q 10 7 5 4

WEST	NORTH	EAST	SOUTH
		1♣	Pass
1♦	Pass	1♠	Pass
4NT	Pass	5♥	Pass
7♠	All pass		

WHAT CAN GO wrong? It's one of my favorite themes.

If you think everything is rosy, stop and ask yourself what can go wrong.

East plays in 7♠. It's a lovely contract. Well bid.

South leads the ♥K, taken by the ace. East counts his tricks and sees that he has:

Four spades
One heart
Six diamonds
One club

That's twelve tricks. Where is the other one coming from? East sees that he can ruff a heart in dummy. Thirteen tricks. It's a good time to ask what can go wrong.

If spades are 5-0, 7♠ will go down. That is a problem you can't avoid. And it's the only problem.

So you have to assume no one has five spades. I will give you a hint. No one has five spades.

Should you draw trump first?

If you lead even one round of trumps, South will show up with four to the eight. Believe it or not, the hand can't be made now. You won't be able to get a heart ruff *and* draw trump. A huge hairy fly will appear in the ointment. South is ruffing diamonds and you won't be able to use the ♦Q as an entry after ruffing a heart. Cruel.

There is a 100% line as long as spades don't divide 5-0. The key is what you do at trick two.

Follow this line. At trick two:

Ruff the ♥J in dummy. No other line of play will succeed (given the 5-0 diamond split).

Play the ♠KQJ. You can win the third round of spades with the ace and can draw the last trump with the nine. Now just cash your winners. At no point can the opponents do anything to harm you.

Hard to see in advance but the ♠9 turned out to be a crucial card.

This is a more difficult hand than most in this book. The theme is to ask yourself if anything can go wrong. This hand is an extreme example of that.

This hand offers one small point in the bidding and one big point in the play. The first point is that these hands will make 7♠ but not 7♦ or 7NT. The key is that the 4-4 fit allows you to ruff a heart in West's hand. In a diamond contract, nothing is gained by ruffing hearts in the West hand since you are ruffing with the long trump holding.

Here is a hypothetical layout that you should worry about. Note that it is unlikely. The odds on a 5-0 diamond split are about 4%. Small, but worth catering to if possible.

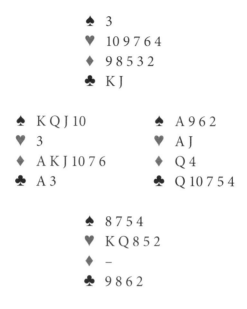

A shame to go down in 7♠. But it was avoidable.
The point of this hand? Reread the first paragraph.

South Deals   +   Both Sides Vulnerable

WEST

♠ 9 4
♥ J 7
♦ A Q 10 6 5
♣ A 9 7 3

WEST	NORTH	EAST	SOUTH
			1♠
?			

THIS HAND OFFERS a lot to think about. The first point is, what should West bid over 1♠?

West should pass. Two-level overcalls need better suits than this. A sixth diamond would be enough for West to bid. If the ♥J was in the diamond suit, the hand would be a marginal 2♦ bid. But the hand West actually has is a clear pass. Remember, West is vulnerable. Vulnerability does count in this game.

	WEST		EAST	
	♠ 9 4		♠ A 10 8 3	
	♥ J 7		♥ Q 10 2	
	♦ A Q 10 6 5		♦ K 7 2	
	♣ A 9 7 3		♣ K Q 2	

WEST	NORTH	EAST	SOUTH
			1♠
Pass	Pass	1NT	Pass
2NT	Pass	3NT	All pass

The second question for this hand is what East should bid when 1♠ is passed to him. You can see that I have East bidding 1NT. Is that OK for you?

Here are some questions about a 1NT bid.

What is your range for a reopening 1NT bid?
Do you promises a stopper in the opened suit?

You can get opinions that say 1NT shows 8–12 points and you can get opinions that it shows 15–18 points. I vote for 12–16.

As for having a stopper in the opponent's suit, you usually do have one. Holdings like 10875 or J83 are marginally acceptable as long as the rest of your hand qualifies.

West raises to 2NT, an invitational bid. East has fourteen with two spade stoppers, and is entitled to bid 3NT.

POSTMORTEM

Note that if East bids 1NT, West can use all of his normal conventions. Stayman and Jacoby transfers and even Texas transfers work here.

For lots more elaboration on this topic, refer to my book *Balancing in Contract Bridge*. Balancing is an important aspect of bidding. If you allow your opponents to buy the contract all of the time, you are missing out on many opportunities.

North Deals + North-South Vulnerable

WEST	EAST
♠ 6 2	♠ K J 9 7 3
♥ J 8 3	♥ 2
♦ Q 10 8 7 6 4	♦ A
♣ 10 5	♣ A Q J 7 6 2

WEST	NORTH	EAST	SOUTH
	1♥	2♣	4♥
Pass	Pass	4♠	Dbl
5♣	Dbl	All pass	

THIS IS ONE of those terrible moments when you have to choose between diving into a pit full of spiders or crawling across a field of snakes. West would love to be somewhere else but sadly, is at a bridge table faced with a scary choice. West has to choose between passing 4♠ doubled and going back to clubs. Since East rates to be 6-5 or 7-5 or even 7-4, it is necessary for West to prefer to 5♣. As bad as it will be, it will be better than 4♠.

It's likely that 5♣ doubled will go down two or three tricks. It is also possible that 4♠ doubled will go down five tricks. When you are about to have a disaster, it's sensible to select the lesser disaster.

POSTMORTEM

A good partner, when putting down this dummy, will make a comment such as, "This is a pathetic hand. I wish I had more." Your partner will appreciate hearing this more than something like this:

"Here we go again. Another zero."

Look at the East hand. East's bidding was certainly sane. If West had three spades to the queen, East might actually make something. Given that West has that hopeless hand, playing in 5♣ doubled may turn out to be a reasonable result because a doubled 4♠ contract may turn out to be worse. We all want to get the best result possible. Sometimes the least-awful result is the best you can do.

QUICKIE

WEST	NORTH	EAST	SOUTH
1♣	1♠	2♣	2♠
3♣	Pass	Pass	?

In a competitive auction, North overcalls 1♠ and South raises. If the auctions continues and South is thinking of bidding 3♠, the most important feature of the hand is a fourth trump.

```
          ♠  Q 6 3
          ♥  Q 6 5 4 2
          ♦  A 6 3
          ♣  7 4
```

Pass.

```
          ♠  Q 6 3 2
          ♥  Q 6 5 3
          ♦  A 3
          ♣  7 6 4
```

Acceptable (barely) to bid 3♠.

South Deals   +   No One Vulnerable

	WEST		EAST
♠	8 7 6 5	♠	K Q 10
♥	7 3	♥	A K
♦	J 9 7 3	♦	Q 8 6 2
♣	7 6 2	♣	Q 10 5 3

WEST	NORTH	EAST	SOUTH
			1♥
Pass	3♥*	?	

*Limit raise

THIS HAND IS a trap for point-counters. Is it worth a takeout double?

This is a case where you can accurately estimate your partner's hand.

East has sixteen high-card points but he has three big flaws. He has only three spades. He has a semi-balanced hand. And, believe it or not, he has the worst possible heart holding. The bidding tells East that West has one or two hearts. There is duplication in hearts, and that is bad. East definitely should pass.

WEST	NORTH	EAST	SOUTH
			1♥
Pass	3♥*	Pass	4♥
Pass	Pass	?	

Should East double 4♥?

East should pass again. East has two heart tricks but he may or may not have a spade trick, and he has hopes for a trick in the minors. West is surely broke so he can't be expected to have anything. Worse, when South bid 4♥, he said he had a good hand. All of this suggests that South expected to make 4♥ when he bid it. It would not be a surprise if South made an overtrick. And don't forget. South might redouble 4♥.

POSTMORTEM

If East doubles 3♥ for takeout, West will bid 3♠. In a spade contract, West has too many losers to count. 3♠ doubled may be down 500 or 800 or even 1100.

The big point of this hand is that East's balanced hand is not worth bidding with after North's limit raise.

East would much prefer to have a hand like this one for a double of 3♥:

$$
\begin{array}{ll}
♠ & \text{K Q 10 2} \\
♥ & \text{3} \\
♦ & \text{Q J 8 7} \\
♣ & \text{A Q 10 2}
\end{array}
$$

This hand, with fourteen high-card points, is worth more than the original sixteen-point hand shown above.

South Deals ✛ East-West Vulnerable

	WEST		EAST
♠	8 2	♠	K Q J 10 4
♥	J 10 9 6 2	♥	3
♦	J 10 6	♦	9 8 2
♣	10 5 4	♣	A J 8 2

WEST	NORTH	EAST	SOUTH
			1NT
Pass	2♣	Pass	2♥
Pass	3NT	Dbl	All pass

WHAT DOES IT MEAN if your opponents bid by themselves to 3NT and your partner ends the bidding with an unexpected double? It's your lead. Obviously, this is an important moment. Is partner doubling on lots of high cards or does he want you to lead a specific suit?

Experts have learned that doubling with some random high cards is not a winning idea. If East had ♠KJ87 ♥QJ4 ♦AQ3 ♣Q73, it would be unwise to double. East knows West has nothing and given that, the chances of taking five tricks on defense are not good. Worse yet, East's double gives away valuable information to declarer.

The treatment here is one I recommend to you. Play that a double by East says that 3NT will go down if West makes the right lead. Usually, East is saying that he wants West to lead the first suit that dummy has bid. (Note that 2♣ was artificial. It is not considered to be a 'bid' suit.) On this auction, North didn't actually 'bid' a suit but his Stayman bid said he had a major and it turned out not to be hearts. It must be spades. If you play that East's double has a special meaning, you should lead a spade. That ♥J is tempting but your partner is making a strong statement. Listen to him and lead the ♠8. Later, I will show a hand that shows a variation on this theme.

POSTMORTEM

East's double is a big winner here. With a spade lead, South can take three hearts, four diamonds, and a spade. He won't have time to get a club trick.

If East doesn't double, West will lead the ♥J. That gives South time to set up two club winners. He will end up taking one spade, three hearts, four diamonds, and two club tricks.

South is down one with a spade lead.

South makes an overtrick with a heart lead.

This is a huge swing.

East's double is the key.

There are other variations of this double. The one shown here is, in my opinion, best. It only requires that partner knows how to interpret it.

QUICKIE

If your partner opens 1NT and you have:

♠ 7 3
♥ J 9 2
♦ 10
♣ J 8 6 5 4 3 2

how do you get to play in clubs? Or do you pass 1NT and hope nothing bad happens?

I'm not suggesting a solution because lots of them exist. I am just checking on your agreements to see if they exist.

South Deals   +   East-West Vulnerable

EAST

♠ A J 4
♥ 3
♦ A 8 3
♣ K 10 8 5 4 3

WEST	NORTH	EAST	SOUTH
			3♥
Dbl	5♥	?	

WEST'S DOUBLE IS takeout. For him to double 3♥, West needs good shape and at least fourteen quality points.

North's jump to 5♥ is a weak bid that forces East to make a very big decision.

He can double or he can bid 6♣. What do you think East should do?

Here's the layout:

WEST	EAST
♠ K 7 6 2	♠ A J 4
♥ 8	♥ 3
♦ K Q 10 9 4	♦ A 8 3
♣ A Q 7	♣ K 10 8 5 4 3

WEST	NORTH	EAST	SOUTH
			3♥
Dbl	5♥	6♣	All pass

East-West can make 6♣ and North-South rate to have seven or eight tricks, so doubling will get you 500 or 800.

Bidding 6♣ is the winning action. But it doesn't have to be. You have to make a decision.

You have two things going for you:

One. Your hand is excellent. In support of clubs you have something like seventeen points. 6♣ will be a good contract much of the time.

Two. This is the kind of auction where your opponents often continue to 6♥. If they do, you double them and get a penalty that's bigger than the players who double 5♥.

POSTMORTEM

Your opponents have put you under pressure here. When this happens, you sometimes need to make a decision you would prefer not to have. This hand is one such. Envision two gladiators fighting in the mud. Oink.

West Deals + East-West Vulnerable

	WEST	EAST	
	♠ 4	♠ Q J 7 3 2	
	♥ A J 10 9 8 6 5	♥ –	
	♦ A J 8 7	♦ K Q 6 3	
	♣ 7	♣ A 9 5 4	

WEST	NORTH	EAST	SOUTH
1♥	Pass	1♠	Pass
2♥	Pass	2NT	Pass
4♥	All pass		

THIS BIDDING LOOKS a little funny. West opened a hand with only ten high-card points with a one-bid. Even vulnerable, this is a good bid. There are many reasons:

West's ten points consist mainly of aces.
West has an excellent suit.
West has superb spot cards.
West has excellent shape.

East's 1♠ bid and West's 2♥ rebid are routine. Curiously, I think the West hand has enough playing strength to rebid 3♥. I wouldn't do this, but it has appeal.

Now we get to East's 2NT bid. Is this really the right call? While you think it over, spend a moment looking at the alternatives. If East passes, a game may be missed. I don't expect anyone to pass, but it could be right. East should never rebid spades. East shouldn't even think of rebidding spades. Rebidding any number of spades shows six (98%). If East bids 3♣ or 3♦, it will be hard to stay short of game. Note that if East bids 3♦ on this hand, West will raise. I think 2NT is the right bid. It shows stoppers in the unbid suits. It shows ten and a half to twelve balanced points. East has a maximum, but he also has a void in hearts. That heart void will be a misery in notrump.

West's final bid is appropriate. East is showing about eleven points and even if East has a singleton heart, West's hearts will play nicely. East turns out to have a void, but the extra spot cards in hearts make up for it.

Note that West didn't rebid a tepid 3♥, leaving East to wonder what to do. This sequence shows good judgment on both sides of the table.

QUICKIE

It is OK to raise partner's 1♥ or 1♠ response with only three trumps if there is nothing better. New players hate to do this. I offer, with every conviction that I can muster, that it is right to raise with three trumps on many occasions. Start now to develop the habit of raising. Do not learn restrictive habits which you will have to unlearn later.

WEST

- ♠ 8 7 3
- ♥ K J 3
- ♦ A Q 9 7
- ♣ 8 4 3

WEST	NORTH	EAST	SOUTH
Pass	Pass	1♥	Pass
?			

PASSED HAND BIDDING is unlike other areas of bidding. It is the one time when a hand can take a light initial action and know that partner will be aware of it.

West passes and East opens 1♥ in third seat. West has a difficult decision. West likes hearts. If East had opened in first or second position, West would bid 1NT, forcing, and then jump to 3♥ showing a 10–11 point raise with three trumps.

He can't do that here because 1NT is not forcing by a passed hand. The solution is to use the Drury convention. For me, it's one of the most important conventions around, yet some players refuse to use it. I consider this a serious error.

West can bid 2♣. This is an artificial bid. 2♣ says responder has a hand too good to raise to 2♥. Opener has a variety of bids available after the Drury bid.

WEST	EAST
♠ 8 7 3	♠ A 10 2
♥ K J 3	♥ Q 9 8 7 5
♦ A Q 9 7	♦ 5 2
♣ 8 4 3	♣ K Q 7

WEST	NORTH	EAST	SOUTH
Pass	Pass	1♥	Pass
2♣	Pass	2♥	All pass

East rebids 2♥ on this hand which says, emphatically, that opener wants to play in 2♥. It's extremely rare for responder to bid again.

Note that 2♥ isn't cold. If East is unlucky, he will lose two spades, two hearts, one diamond, and two clubs. Could happen. On the other side of the coin, East will make three if he is lucky. Best by far is to stop in 2♥.

POSTMORTEM

An important reminder: Responder should never jump-raise 1♥ or 1♠ to the three level without four or more trumps and proper values. This applies after opening bids in any seat.

For those of you who are having trouble with passed hand sequences, I have a book on the topic entitled *The Complete Guide to Passed Hand Bidding*. It contains a lot of practical advice as well as some advanced ideas late in the book.

As noted above, I am aware that some players don't like lots of conventions. I recommend that you make an exception for Drury. It's a convention you will forget just once. Nothing reinforces a convention like a 'forget'.

South Deals + North-South Vulnerable

	WEST		EAST
♠	K 10 7 3	♠	J 9 6 4
♥	Q J 6 3 2	♥	5
♦	Q 8	♦	A J 7 3 2
♣	10 4	♣	A Q 7

WEST	NORTH	EAST	SOUTH
			1♥
Pass	Pass	Dbl	Pass
1♠	Pass	2♠	All pass

THERE ARE TWO decisions of note here. East's reopening double is routine. West has the first real decision. Should West pass for penalty, or bid 1♠?

I have a rule for such situations. If I am not positive that playing for penalties is correct, I bid if I have something good to bid. Both conditions are met here. West has five hearts, but he has few values on the side. East's double could be light in the reopening seat, so even with this hand, 1♥ doubled might make. Secondly, West has four spades, which East has asked for. Bidding 1♠ makes perfect sense.

The second decision is East's. This isn't a good enough hand to make an immediate double of 1♥ and then to raise spades. But it is good enough to make a balancing double of 1♥ and then to compete to 2♠.

What happens if West passes? He has to lead something. Any lead West makes may work poorly.

Here's the layout:

```
                    ♠  Q 5
                    ♥  8 7
                    ♦  10 9 6 5
                    ♣  9 6 5 3 2

♠  K 10 7 3                          ♠  J 9 6 4
♥  Q J 6 3 2                         ♥  5
♦  Q 8                               ♦  A J 7 3 2
♣  10 4                              ♣  A Q 7

                    ♠  A 8 2
                    ♥  A K 10 9 4
                    ♦  K 4
                    ♣  K J 8
```

Say West reasonably leads a spade. Declarer would win the queen and would lead a diamond towards his hand. No matter how East defends, South will get two spade tricks and a spade ruff, a diamond, and he can't be stopped from getting three heart tricks. Other leads are not successful. An overtrick is possible if the defense strays.

West should make 2♠ without sweating. This result is a good example of the fact that defending is harder than declaring. If given a choice, playing a hand is the easy decision.

POSTMORTEM

One of the considerations for West is the quality of his hearts. ♥QJ632 is not as good as ♥QJ986. West would be happier to pass with better hearts.

The difference in value is huge.

HAND

39

BIDDING OVER A preempt is not a good way to make a living. There is a useful guideline I can offer that will help with these decisions. It is called the Rule of Seven.

THE RULE OF SEVEN

If you bid a suit over a preempt, you are entitled to hope your partner has seven ordinary points with a tolerance for your suit. If your hand is good enough that your bid will be 'safe' facing this seven-point hand, you can make that bid.

If you double a preempt, you are entitled to hope your partner will have seven ordinary points and a four-card unbid suit to bid. If your hand is good enough that a double will be safe facing this seven-point hand, you can double.

Say your RHO opens 2♥. Can you overcall with this hand?

♠ Q 8 7 6 3
♥ K 5
♦ K 7 3
♣ K J 7

It's worth about twelve points. It has a poor spade suit. Not beautiful. If your partner has seven ordinary points, your side has nineteen. Here's a hand he might have with seven ordinary points:

♠ 9 4 2   ♠ Q 8 7 6 3
♥ J 8 4   ♥ K 5
♦ Q 5 4 2   ♦ K 7 3
♣ A 8 6   ♣ K J 7

These two hands have two to five spade losers. One heart loser. Perhaps two diamond losers. Perhaps one club loser. Not good at all if 2♠ is doubled.

The following hand includes bidding situations where an opponent preempts. You are South.

WEST	NORTH	EAST	SOUTH
3♦	?	Pass	?

♠ Q 8
♥ K 7 3
♦ A 9 2
♣ 10 9 7 6 3

What do you respond when your partner, North, makes one of the following bids? In all cases, your RHO passes. On this hand you have some nice values. It is not always the case. You can have better, you can have worse.

1. Partner doubles
2. Partner bids 3♥
3. Partner bids 3NT
4. Partner bids 4♦
5. Partner bids 4♠

ANSWERS

1. When partner doubles
   It is reasonable to bid 3NT and hope it makes. Bidding 4♣ isn't terrible, but it doesn't show values. You would bid 4♣ with much worse hands.
2. When partner bids 3♥
   You have more than the seven points partner 'hopes for' and you have good heart support. This is a clear raise to 4♥.

3. When partner bids 3NT

   Pass. Not an easy bid at all. Partner's 3NT bid shows anything from a balanced fifteen-count up to a 25-count that isn't suited to anything else. Usually partner has 16–20 and a pass works out best for you. It isn't worth trying for the brass ring.

4. When partner bids 4♦

   Partner is using a Michaels bid to show the majors, and since you are at the four level, he must have a fine hand. 4♥ is the obvious bid but you could be missing something good. Take full credit if you bid 4♥ and felt like bidding more.

5. When partner bids 4♠

   This is a strong jump overcall. It shows more than a 3♠ overcall. He expects to make 4♠ opposite an ordinary seven-count. This hand is good enough that you can make a gentle slam try with 5♦. Your hand is worth a lot more than seven points. You upgrade good cards and downgrade bad cards. The ♦Q would be downgraded to zero. Your ♠Q is enormous. It gets upgraded. It's certainly worth more than two points. Remember. You have this card, not one of the opponents. Your ♥K looks good too. It could be worth more than three points. And your ♦A is solid. I'd rate this hand at about twelve points.

HAND 40

WEST	NORTH	EAST	SOUTH
3♥	?	Pass	?

♠ 9 8 6 4 2
♥ 9 3
♦ A 8
♣ K J 7 2

What do you respond when your partner, North, makes one of the following bids? Your RHO passes.

1. When partner doubles
2. When partner bids 3♠
3. When partner bids 3NT
4. When partner bids 4♣

ANSWERS

1. When partner doubles
   A simple hand. Bid 4♠. Partner's double is takeout and even though he may have only three spades, you have lots more than the guideline rule of seven points suggests. Your partner would double 1♥ with some hands with twelve support points. He needs about sixteen support points to double 3♥.
2. When partner bids 3♠
   You are lucky your RHO didn't bid something. You have a wonderful hand for partner. You can raise to 4♠.

3. When partner bids 3NT

   Pass and be pleased that you have some high cards. Remember that partner's 3NT bid is undefined.

4. When partner bids 4♣

   Assume your partner's 4♣ bid is natural. Some players use it as something else. Natural four-level overcalls in a minor suit show very good hands with lots of shape. You have much more than seven points in support of a club contract. Raise to 5♣.

IT'S BAD ENOUGH when an opponent pre-empts against you. Your LHO opens, say, 2♠ and your partner doubles. You have to make your first bid at the three level and sometimes you have to make your bid with no high cards at all. Could things be worse?

Yes. They could. If your RHO raises opener's preempt, you may have to make your first bid at the four or five level. Admittedly, if you have a hopeless hand, you can pass. But if you have a hand with a few values and a fair suit, you have to decide whether or not to enter the bidding. There is a convention known as the responsive double that will help on auctions where partner doubles and RHO raises.

WEST	NORTH	EAST	SOUTH
2♦	Dbl	3♦	?

NO ONE VULNERABLE

1. ♠ K 10 6 3
   ♥ 8 3
   ♦ 8 7 3
   ♣ A J 9 4

2. ♠ 8 2
   ♥ Q 10 6 5 4 2
   ♦ 7 4
   ♣ 10 5 4

3. ♠ K 2
   ♥ 8 7 3
   ♦ 7 6 3
   ♣ A J 10 7 4

4. ♠ Q 8 5
   ♥ J 8 6 3
   ♦ Q 10 5
   ♣ K 3 2

5. ♠ Q J 6 2
   ♥ K 10 8 6
   ♦ 7 6 2
   ♣ Q 10

6. ♠ K Q J 7 4
   ♥ A 3
   ♦ 4 3
   ♣ J 8 7 4

1. ♠ K 10 6 3
   ♥ 8 3
   ♦ 8 7 3
   ♣ A J 9 4

Bid 3♠. You have only four spades, but the quality of your points makes up for this. Use the Rule of Seven to help guide you. When your RHO raises his partner's preempt, you can be a bit more aggressive to make a bid. You do this because you need to let partner know you have something. Here, you have nine support points so are entitled to bid 3♠. If you don't bid, your side may get shut out of the auction. That might be expensive. You have to fight back a bit in this situation. Of course, if you have only five boring points or less, you are allowed to pass. This hand is slightly better than needed to bid here.

2. ♠ 8 2
   ♥ Q 10 6 5 4 2
   ♦ 7 4
   ♣ 10 5 4

Pass. You have good playing strength but terrible high cards. If you can make 4♥, your partner will be able to double again. Too bad you can't bid 3♥ and have everyone else pass. If you felt the urge to bid 3♥, you get some credit.

3. ♠ K 2
   ♥ 8 7 3
   ♦ 7 6 3
   ♣ A J 10 7 4

Try 4♣. Your fifth club plus the ♣10 make this a reasonable bid. Note that with diamonds bid and raised, your three little diamonds become an asset. Having three of them increases the chances that your partner has a singleton. It's interesting how three little in an opponent's suit is initially a terrible holding, and how good three little becomes when opener's partner raises.

4. ♠ Q 8 5
   ♥ J 8 6 3
   ♦ Q 10 5
   ♣ K 3 2

Pass. Even though you have eight high-card points, they are bad points. Your ♦Q is worthless and your shape stinks. This hand is way worse than the seven points partner is hoping you have.

5. ♠ Q J 6 2
   ♥ K 10 8 6
   ♦ 7 6 2
   ♣ Q 10

If you are a fan of responsive doubles, you will recognize that this hand qualifies. You have just the right values for a responsive double. Four-four in the majors and eight useful points is perfect. If not using responsive doubles, I would feel strapped for a good bid.

6. ♠ K Q J 7 4
   ♥ A 3
   ♦ 4 3
   ♣ J 8 7 4

Bid 4♠. Bidding 3♠ is feeble. Considering that it was right to bid 3♠ on Hand 1 above, you must do more with this one. You have an opening bid (of sorts) opposite a hand that could double at the two level. The important thing here is that if you bid 4♠, your partner will appreciate that you are bidding the full value of your hand. If you bid 3♠, he knows you have a lesser hand than this.

QUICKIE

- How many points do you show when you double a strong (15–17) notrump?
- How many points do you show when you double a weak (12–14) notrump?

Curiously, you should have almost as good a hand to double a weak notrump as you need to double a strong notrump. When you double a strong notrump, you need a wonderful fifteen points or more. When you double a weak notrump, you should have a fair fifteen points or more.

It is easier to say this than it is to explain. The reason is that if you double a strong notrump when you have sixteen points, you know that your high cards will be over declarer's high cards. That will work well for you defensively. If you double a weak notrump with a thirteen-point hand, there is a greater chance that dummy will have some points and your points will be sandwiched between them. It's true that your side may have half of the deck, but declarer will have the big advantage of playing the hand while you are defending it. You will learn the hard way, if you haven't already, that defense is much more difficult than playing the dummy.

| | HAND 42 | West Deals | + | East-West Vulnerable |

	WEST	EAST
♠	K Q 3	♠ A 7 6
♥	K 3	♥ A Q J 4
♦	K 7 4	♦ A 8 3
♣	A K 8 7 4	♣ Q J 2

WEST	NORTH	EAST	SOUTH
1♣	Pass	1♥	Pass
2NT	Pass	4♣	Pass
4♥	Pass	5♣	Pass
5♥	Pass	7NT	All pass

THE AUCTION STARTS easily with the first three bids. East, who has an amazingly good hand under the circumstances, tries Gerber. Even when clubs have already been bid, a jump over notrump to 4♣ is Gerber. West shows one ace with 4♥ (1 or 4). East continues with 5♣. 5♥ (1 or 4) says he has zero kings or all four of them. East knows it has to be all four, so bids the grand slam. It will make if West has five clubs or if West has a queen, or finally, if West has a jack and can take a winning finesse. On this hand 7NT would make if West had just four clubs.

POSTMORTEM

Some players use a different set of answers to Gerber or Blackwood than those shown here. The important thing is that East is able to get enough information to bid 7NT.

East Deals + Both Sides Vulnerable

THIS BIDDING SITUATION comes up every day. The seven hands here offer thoughts on how to handle some of the more obscure problems.

WEST	NORTH	EAST	SOUTH
		1♣	?

1. ♠ A Q J 8
   ♥ 7 3
   ♦ 9 8
   ♣ A Q 5 4 2

2. ♠ 7 3
   ♥ 3
   ♦ A J 9 8 7 5
   ♣ J 9 8 6

3. ♠ Q 7 6 5 2
   ♥ K 8 7 5 2
   ♦ 3
   ♣ K 7

4. ♠ J 10 6
   ♥ A K J 8
   ♦ A Q 7 2
   ♣ 8 2

5. ♠ Q 8 7 3
   ♥ A Q
   ♦ K J 7 6
   ♣ Q 10 7

6. ♠ A K J 8 7
   ♥ A Q 7
   ♦ K J 2
   ♣ 10 6

7. ♠ 4 2
   ♥ A Q 9 7 5
   ♦ A K Q 7
   ♣ 8 3

ANSWERS

1. Bid 1♠. Now and then you can overcall with a four-card suit. Four-card-suit overcalls require all of the following:
   1. A very good suit
   2. One level only
   3. A good hand. Thirteen useful points or so
   4. You do not have a better bid, such as a takeout double.

   1♠ is both constructive and very obstructive to your opponents. If you're able to bid 1♦, you should realize that it is not obstructive.

2. Pass. You are vulnerable so this is not sufficient for a bid. If you were not vulnerable, bidding 2♦ would be fine. Note that a 2♦ bid makes it hard for West to show one or both majors.

3. Pass. A Michaels cuebid shows more than this when vulnerable. Add the ♥J and ♠J and it's acceptable to bid 2♣. You have to have agreements on what a minimum Michaels hand shows. I suggest a decent eight high-card points not vulnerable, and a tad more if you are vulnerable. I am aware that some players are much more aggressive.

4. Double. You have the shape for a takeout double. Do not get lost in overcalling with this good four-card heart suit. Note that is is acceptable to have just three cards in a major (spades, here).

5. Pass. Not enough to bid 1NT, too poor a spade suit to bid 1♠, and not nearly enough to double and then bid notrump when partner bids hearts.

6. Double. This is the minimum you should have to double and bid a suit. You need a good hand because the opponents can sometimes raise the bidding, making it expensive for you to show your suit later.

7. Bid 1♥ and expect to show diamonds later. This is not good enough for a double first.

East Deals + **No One Vulnerable**

WEST	NORTH	EAST	SOUTH
		3♥	?

ONE OF THE more annoying problems comes when your RHO bids three of a suit and you have a good hand that doesn't offer a takeout double or an overcall. The following hands include ideas about what to do when you are hit with a well-timed pre-empt. In this case, your RHO opens with 3♥.

1. ♠ 7 4
   ♥ A J 10
   ♦ K Q J 9 7
   ♣ K Q 7

2. ♠ A Q J
   ♥ K 8 3
   ♦ A K J 8
   ♣ A Q 10

3. ♠ A K
   ♥ K 3
   ♦ A K J 9 8 7 5
   ♣ 5 4

4. ♠ A 2
   ♥ A K J 9
   ♦ J 3
   ♣ A Q 9 8 7

5. ♠ 6 3
   ♥ A Q
   ♦ K Q J 10 5 4
   ♣ Q J 3

6. ♠ A 3
   ♥ 8 3
   ♦ A K Q 10 7 6 5
   ♣ A 8

7. ♠ A J
   ♥ 6 4 2
   ♦ K Q 7 5 4
   ♣ A K 8

ANSWERS

1. Bid 3NT. East's bid has made life hard. If your partner can produce a few points, you rate to have a good play for 3NT. This is a routine bid. Yes, you have two small spades. It's a sensible risk to take. Your partner is likely to have enough spades to stop the opponents from running the suit.

2. Bid 3NT. This time you have a mountain. But what else can you do? If you double, your partner will often bid 4♣ or 4♦, and now you are beyond your likely best contract of 3NT.

3. Bid 3NT. If you bid 4♦ and make it, you get 130. If you bid 3NT and make it, you get 400. In either contract, you will need a little luck.

4. Bid 3NT. It would be nice to double 3♥ for penalty but that's not what a double means. If you pass, that will likely end the bidding and you will get 150 or so for down three. If you bid 3NT and make it, quite likely, you will get a game bonus.

5. Bid 3NT. Yes, 3NT again. With the expected heart lead, you will set up the diamonds and hope for some help from partner. Obviously, this bid doesn't have to work.

6. Bid 5♦. This is a strong bid, not a preemptive bid. You have nine tricks but bidding 3NT just doesn't feel right. Bid 5♦, hoping that your partner has something like the KQ2 of spades or clubs. It's a logical choice. The big deal here is that if you bid 4♦, your partner won't know how little you need for game. He would pass many hands that give you a shot at game.

7. Pass. As annoying as the previous hand was, at least you had a bid you could make. This hand is tougher. You have a nice seventeen points that offers no sane bid.

POSTMORTEM

These hands demonstrate that a 3NT overcall is not well defined. The hands here range from fifteen points (Hand 5) up to 24 points (Hand 2).

They also show that some good hands are unexpectedly awkward or even impossible to bid.

QUICKIE

If you open and partner responds at the two level:

1♠   2♦

a new suit by you at the three level:

1♠   2♦
3♣

shows a good hand. Do not make this rebid with a twelve- or thirteen-point hand. Partner is entitled to expect an ace more than a minimum opening bid. With:

♠   Q J 7 4 3
♥   K 7 3
♦   8
♣   A Q 8 3

you should rebid 2♠ over partner's 2♦ bid. Do not bid 2NT and do not bid 3♣. 2NT promises two or more diamonds and 3♣ promises a much bigger hand.

IMPORTANT THOUGHT

Some players feel that rebidding 2♠ promises six cards. If you agree, then you will also agree that there is no good rebid with this hand. I strongly suggest you do not promise six cards here.

North Deals   +   Both Sides Vulnerable

	WEST		EAST
♠	2	♠	9 8
♥	Q J 8 7 3	♥	10
♦	A K 5	♦	9 8 3
♣	Q 10 9 2	♣	A K J 8 7 6 4

WEST	NORTH	EAST	SOUTH
	Pass	3♣	3♥
5♣	Dbl	All pass	

WEST MUST NOT double 3♥. He can set it but it won't be played there. North will predictably bid spades, which isn't what West wants. By bidding 5♣, West gets to a spot that has a play and makes it difficult for North to bid spades.

Can you make 5♣?

Probably not. Importantly, their side can make 5♠ and they will probably bid it. East-West will get two diamonds but no clubs.

QUICKIE

If you have a preemptive hand and an opponent opens with a strong 2♣ bid, go ahead and preempt anyway if you aren't vulnerable. The 2♣ bidder will not appreciate the loss of bidding space.

South Deals + No One Vulnerable

	WEST		EAST
♠	A 9 7 6 2	♠	K 5 3
♥	Q J	♥	A 9 6 3 2
♦	K 10 7 4	♦	8
♣	K 8	♣	Q 10 7 5

WEST	NORTH	EAST	SOUTH
			1♦
1♠	Pass	2♦	3♦
Dbl	All pass		

WEST OVERCALLS AND East, with too much for a simple raise, makes a cuebid. East intends to pass if West rebids 2♠. When South rebids 3♦, West has a chance for a super bid, and doubles 3♦.

If you think this bid is obvious, I promise you that many players miss this kind of chance when the hand is played. They count up their points and decide to bid 3♠. Here's the entire hand:

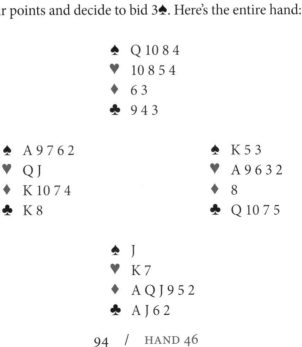

I will let the result speak for itself. South is down two or three in 3♦. West would be down at least one in 3♠.

POSTMORTEM

There is a valuable consideration that West must be aware of in the bidding. East's cuebid almost always shows exactly three trumps and ten or more support points. East will have four trumps so rarely that it's not worth worrying about.

When East has three trumps, the East-West hands will play less well than if East has four trumps. If East has four trumps and limit raise values, he jumps to 3♦ to show his four trumps and better shape. Note that this is not a splinter bid.

QUICKIE

Don't double the opponents' cuebids or their artificial bids when they are going to slam unless you think your partner is going to be on opening lead. If he is the leader, he may need your double to help him. If you are going to be on opening lead, you don't want to tell the opponents something that may help them.

North Deals   +   North-South Vulnerable

WEST	NORTH	EAST	SOUTH
	Pass	Pass	1NT
Pass	4♥	Pass	4♠
All pass			

♠ J 10 8 6 5 4 2
♥ K 8 2
♦ 6 3 2
♣ –

♠ K 9
♥ A J 7
♦ J 8 7 4
♣ A K J 6

THIS HAND SHOWS why blunt bidding is often best. For starters, North didn't preempt. The suit and hand are not good enough, vulnerable. When South opened 1NT, North made a transfer bid of 4♥, getting the play into the South hand.

Looking at both hands, you can see that it is easy to beat 4♠. A diamond lead will set 4♠ one or two tricks. Does this mean you are in a hopeless contract?

Not at all. Here are the East-West hands:

	WEST		EAST
♠	Q	♠	A 7 3
♥	10 9 6 4	♥	Q 5 3
♦	A Q 10	♦	K 9 5
♣	10 9 7 5 3	♣	Q 8 4 2

West will never lead a spade and he definitely won't lead a diamond, the killing lead. He will probably remember that North didn't double 4♥ for a heart lead and will settle on the ♣10.

How nice. Goodbye, three diamond losers.

Now you have a play for six!

POSTMORTEM

Defenders are not omniscient. You will get away with a lot of 'unmakeable' contracts for the reason that defenders are human and will make many unlucky leads and plays. West's club lead into South's ♣AKJ6 cost the defense three tricks.

QUICKIE

Don't play a new convention until you know how it works. There is more to a convention than just knowing its name. It is one thing to say that an opening 2♦ bid is weak showing 6–10 points. You still have to know what it means when your partner responds and what it means when you rebid. Incidentally, don't give up on a convention just because someone forgets it. (At first, someone will forget it. It is just a matter of who goofs first.)

West Deals + No One Vulnerable

WEST		EAST	
♠ K J 10 7 5		♠ A 9 6 4 2	
♥ A 6 4		♥ 8 5	
♦ 9 8		♦ A K 10 5	
♣ K J 10		♣ A 7	

WEST	NORTH	EAST	SOUTH
1♠	Dbl	2NT	Pass
3♠	Pass	4♣	Pass
4♥	Pass	4NT	Pass
5♥	Pass	6♠	All pass

A GOOD AUCTION using conventions and judgment. East's 2NT bid shows a limit raise or better. It's called the Jordan raise. West expects that East has a limit raise and rebids 3♠, a sign-off bid.

Now East redefines his hand. If East had game-going points only, he would bid 4♠. With a hand good enough to look for a slam facing a minimum opening bid, he cuebids 4♣.

Back to West. West showed a minimum hand but in that context, the one he has isn't bad. He cuebids the ♥A, confident that East won't expect more.

East asks for keycards and puts it in a slam. Might make an overtrick.

POSTMORTEM

When West draws trump, he should consider that if either defender has a void in spades, it will be North, the takeout doubler.

North Deals   +   No One Vulnerable

WEST	EAST
♠ A K 7 3	♠ J 9 4
♥ 10 7 6 3	♥ A Q J 5
♦ Q 9 4	♦ A K 8 3 2
♣ 10 7	♣ 8

WEST	NORTH	EAST	SOUTH
	3♣	Dbl	4♣
Dbl	Pass	4♥	All pass

LOTS OF UNDERSTANDINGS used in this sequence. East doubles for takeout. In order to bid at the three level, he needs about sixteen support points, which is what he has. When South raises to 4♣, West knows he has enough to look for a major-suit fit. The way to do that is to double. This is the responsive double. Some partnerships don't play them at this level. I think that this hand answers that objection. By doubling, West lets East know he is to bid a major. Holding four hearts and five diamonds, East bids hearts. He does not think of bidding diamonds because West's double didn't ask for them.

The responsive double gets East-West to their eight-card heart fit. Had West guessed which major to bid he might have chosen spades, and that would be a scary contract.

	WEST	EAST	
♠	Q 10 7 6	♠ J 5 4 2	
♥	A J 6 3	♥ K 4	
♦	2	♦ J 8 6	
♣	K 10 9 8	♣ A Q 5 3	

WEST	NORTH	EAST	SOUTH
Pass	2♦	Pass	3♦
Dbl	Pass	3♠	All pass

THIS IS A theme you need to know about. It has to do with balancing. West passes and hears North open a weak 2♦ bid. East is nowhere near finding a bid. South raises to 3♦, posing a problem for West. West finds a takeout double. Here's why he can get away with it.

He has the right shape.

He is a passed hand so can't have a full opening bid.

He expects from South's simple raise that East has something.

Finally, West knows that if he passes, East won't have the shape to bid and the opponents will likely steal the hand for 3♦.

East has a good hand with fitting honors for all suits and he has a nice four-card spade suit. With West being a passed hand, though, East is content to bid 3♠ knowing West has a maximum of eleven or so points. As it is, East might make 4♠ but bringing in nine tricks should be a good result. Note that North rates to make 3♦, which would be a terrible result for East-West.

South Deals + No One Vulnerable

WEST	EAST
♠ K	♠ J 9 6 5 4 3
♥ A K J 8 7	♥ 2
♦ Q 6 3	♦ J 10 7 4
♣ A J 7 3	♣ 9 5

WEST	NORTH	EAST	SOUTH
			1♣
1♥	All pass		

ONE HEART GOES down one and 1♠ makes. Did we do badly? We did not. If East bids 1♠, West will go to 2NT at the least and might bid three. That will be a disaster and it might be doubled. 4♠ would definitely be doubled. Remember that a bid by East promises something. 1♠ would not be forcing, but it should not be bid on a hand with two jacks.

The best plan is to pass and if the chance arises, bid 1♠ later. This can happen if South doubles 1♥ and North passes.

QUICKIE

Learn the proprieties. An ethical player gets more respect than an unethical one. You hate it when an opponent 'loud doubles' you. Your opponents don't like it either.

South Deals   +   Both Sides Vulnerable

WEST	EAST
♠ 10	♠ Q J 9 8 5
♥ J	♥ 9 8
♦ K J 8 7 2	♦ A 3
♣ A Q 7 5 4 3	♣ K 9 8 2

WEST	NORTH	EAST	SOUTH
			1♥
2NT	3♥	4♣	4♥
5♣	All pass		

WEST BIDS 2NT, unusual. A fine bid. This convention is often abused. Not this time. East is the one with the first problem. To bid or not to bid?

With two important minor-suit high cards, East should bid 4♣. West did make a vulnerable 2NT bid. He must have had a reason to do so.

If East bids 4♣, West will bid five on the basis of his extra good shape. Both 4♥ and 5♣ will make.

POSTMORTEM

Some interesting facts about the unusual notrump:

- People tend to make too many unusual 2NT bids.
- Responder tends to underbid after partner's 2NT bid.
- The 2NT bidder tends to overbid a lot.

Do you?

South Deals   +   East-West Vulnerable

WEST	EAST
♠ 4	♠ Q J 10 9 7 5
♥ J 10 8 2	♥ A 7 3
♦ Q J 5	♦ 8 7 3
♣ 9 8 6 3 2	♣ A

WEST	NORTH	EAST	SOUTH
			1NT
Pass	2NT	Pass	3NT
Pass	Pass	Dbl	All pass

EAST HAS A chance to make two excellent bids. First, East passes over 2NT. He knows West is weak, and that adds up to down two or three if East bids 3♠. Best is to pass. When South goes on to game, East can double. This is a special bid that says East is hoping for a good lead from West. Usually, East has a good suit and wants West to guess what it is.

West looks at his hand and sensibly determines that East has a spade suit, and so leads the ♠4. Leading a singleton against 3NT is usually hopeless but here, it is dictated by East's double. Today, East's double beats 3NT two tricks when it might have made an overtrick had he not doubled. West would lead a club or a heart, which gives declarer needed timing.

POSTMORTEM

East's double is the Lightner lead-directing double. It's well known when used against slams. Interestingly, it can be used on more occasions such as the one above.

West Deals + No One Vulnerable

WEST	EAST
♠ A K J 5	♠ Q 7 4
♥ J 7 2	♥ Q 9 8 4
♦ 2	♦ Q 8 6 5 3
♣ A K Q 7 2	♣ 8

WEST	NORTH	EAST	SOUTH
1♣	Pass	1♥	Pass
1♠	All pass		

WEST PLAYS IN 1♠. Is this OK?

It is. East properly responded 1♥, not 1♦. Almost always it is right to show your hearts before showing your diamonds.

Look at the West hand. Even with a mountain, West rebid just 1♠. The idea is simple enough. If East passes 1♠, he must have a useless hand. You're unlikely to miss a game if East doesn't keep bidding over 1♠.

If West rebids 2♠, East will bid 2NT because the jump is forcing. West will continue with 3♥ and by now the partnership is skating on thin ice. East most likely will bid 3NT, which will fail barring a miracle or bad defense.

East Deals + North-South Vulnerable

♠ A 5
♥ J 10 3
♦ K 4 2
♣ 10 8 6 5 2

♠ K 9 4
♥ K 6 4
♦ 10 9 6 5
♣ A K 4

♠ Q J 10 8 7 3
♥ 2
♦ Q J 7 3
♣ 9 3

♠ 6 2
♥ A Q 9 8 7 5
♦ A 8
♣ Q J 7

WEST	NORTH	EAST	SOUTH
		2♠	3♥
3♠	4♥	?	

HERE'S A HAND from my files in which an opponent does something pretty bad. Would you make the error made on this hand?

East opened 2♠. South bid 3♥ and West, 3♠. When North bid 4♥, East decided to save in 4♠. How did this work out?

East bid 4♠ contrary to one of the most basic rules of bridge, and got whacked for his troubles. 4♠ went down two when the defenders got a diamond ruff, and that cost 300.

This would be OK if 4♥ makes, but does it?

It turns out that routine defense sets it not one, but two tricks. West leads clubs, giving East a third round ruff. East returns a spade and declarer still has a heart and a spade to lose.

East's decision to bid 4♠ is one of the worst kinds of bids. He preempted, telling his partner that he had six spades and some number of points. West knows what East has. East doesn't know what West has. For all East knows, West bid 3♠ hoping to push North-South to 4♥.

East's correct bid over 4♥ is pass, and it should be made without any mental struggling at all. When you preempt, you should pass for the rest of the auction unless your partner has clearly asked you for an opinion.

On this auction, West did not ask for East's opinion about anything.

This result is bad for the partnership. West won't forget it soon.

QUICKIE

Learn to accept background aggravations. The world is not perfect. The room may be too hot, the computer may have gone berserk, the kibitzer may have had garlic bread with lunch. Ignore these things. Deal with the bridge issues. No excuses!!

West Deals   +   No One Vulnerable

WEST	EAST
♠ K J 10 7 5 2	♠ 6
♥ 7 2	♥ K Q J 5
♦ 9 3	♦ K J 7 4
♣ Q 7 2	♣ A J 6 3

WEST	NORTH	EAST	SOUTH
2♠	All pass		

IT'S CLEAR FOR West to open 2♠ and clear for East to pass. East has good values but the singleton spade is not good for notrump. 3NT, predictably, has little chance. East's best bet is to pass. If South balances, their side will be in jeopardy.

One thing that East must learn is not to spend time suffering over 2♠ before passing. Letting the opponents know you have a good hand is a good way to nudge them out of your trap.

QUICKIE

Don't be afraid to ask for a clear explanation of an alert. But do so at your turn and only do so if you feel you need to know the explanation. Don't ask just to make noise. The opponents may get more out of the explanation than you. Remember, you can always ask at the end of the auction.

West Deals + No One Vulnerable

WEST	NORTH	EAST	SOUTH
1♦	Dbl	2♦	?

1. ♠ 10 8 5 4 3
   ♥ Q 10 5
   ♦ 8 7 3
   ♣ K 4

2. ♠ 6 3
   ♥ Q 9 8 4
   ♦ J 7 5 3
   ♣ A 7 2

3. ♠ Q 9 6
   ♥ J 10 4
   ♦ Q J 5 4
   ♣ K 4 3

4. ♠ Q 7
   ♥ Q 10 5 4 3
   ♦ 8 7 6 3
   ♣ A 7

ONE OF THE most potent areas of competitive bidding is responding to partner's takeout double. When partner doubles for takeout, he is offering three suits for your inspection. The chances are good that you have a fit and if you have a few points too, the hand may belong to your side. There is no area of bidding where it is so incumbent on you to get involved.

What do you do with the four hands above?

HAND 1. Bid 2♠. This is not a close decision. You have five high-card points in the suits partner is asking for and you have a five-card major. That's huge. Given that partner is showing at least three spades and is likely to have four, you have a clear bid.

HAND 2. Bid 2♥. True, you have only four hearts, but partner said he had hearts with you. If your partner overcalled 1♥, you would raise. You should treat this auction more or less the same. Note that your partner has at least three-card support. If your partner likes to double without support for all suits, you will want to discuss it with him.

Here's my often repeated warning: If you don't bid when you reasonably can, you will lose many good results. Passing is not good bridge. Note that your partner will be very wary about raising you with three hearts.

HAND 3. When partner makes a takeout double, you should fight to bid when you have a suit. When you have something like this hand, nine high-card points notwithstanding, you should pass. Bidding notrump is your only option and it's probably a losing one. Bid with fits. Points are less important.

HAND 4. Bid 3♥. This is invitational, not forcing. You show in the range of nine to eleven points. Your hand is at the top of this range. You may have five hearts, you may have four.

When I show this hand during a class on takeout doubles, around 60% of the class bid just 2♥. Consider that if it is right to bid 2♥ on Hand 2, then this hand is surely worth a stronger bid. Given Hand 4 has five hearts, good shape, and cards in suits your partner likes, I rate this hand as worth four support points more than Hand 2.

West Deals + North-South Vulnerable

WEST	NORTH	EAST	SOUTH
1♦	Dbl	1NT	?

1. ♠ Q 6 2
   ♥ J 10 6 5 4 2
   ♦ 7 6 2
   ♣ 8

2. ♠ 7 3
   ♥ K 8 3
   ♦ 7 6 3
   ♣ Q 10 9 6 2

3. ♠ J 9 6
   ♥ Q 7 6 3
   ♦ Q 3 2
   ♣ Q 6 2

4. ♠ K 8 7 4
   ♥ K 4 3
   ♦ 7 6 3
   ♣ K 9 6

THIS AUCTION AND the previous auction have similar themes. When partner makes a takeout double, your right hand opponent often bids something. This is, as they say, your last chance to shine. If you do not bid, the bidding will often be too high for you to have second thoughts.

Most players will have around 8–9 high-card points for their 1NT bid. You should be willing to compete but with modest caution.

HAND 1. Bid 2♥. In support of hearts, you have close to eight points. Remember that you have a fit. Your long hearts are gold. Length in a major when partner makes a takeout double is one of the best things you can have. The ♠Q is nice and the stiff club is also a plus.

HAND 2. The same principle. Bid 2♣. You should be a little cautious about bidding a minor suit in this situation because your partner might fudge a little on club support. Still, worrying is a losing habit. Note that if you pass and opener bids, say, 2♦, you will have to bid 3♣ if you want to change your mind.

HAND 3. Pass. It's OK to bid a four-card major freely, but doing so should show more useful points. The ♦Q is probably worthless and your shape is poor. If you had five hearts, bidding would be sensible. Compare this hand with the first hand. The first one, with its good distribution and long suit, is worth much more than Hand 3, which has twice as many high-card points.

HAND 4. Bid 2♠. Don't let your shape stop you from bidding. You have solid values. If they compete to the three level, let your partner decide whether to go further.

HAND 59

ONE OF THE odder errors that I see is failure to double. On the other side of the coin, I see bad doubles. This discussion talks about both. Here are some examples:

WEST	NORTH	EAST	SOUTH
		1♥	Pass
3♥	Pass	4♣	?

WEST'S 3♥ BID was a limit raise, promising four hearts or more. East's 4♣ bid was a cuebid. East is looking for a slam.

What do you bid with this South hand?

♠ Q J 5 4
♥ 3
♦ J 5 4
♣ K J 9 8 7

I've seen players in this situation double. For penalty.

This is bad. It's impulsive and ultimately, silly. East isn't going to play in clubs. He's going to play in some number of hearts. Why tell declarer that you have good clubs? Let him find out in the play, not during the bidding. Further, you need to realize that this double won't help your partner in any way. You will be on lead. Not him.

WEST	NORTH	EAST	SOUTH
		1♥	Pass
2♥	Pass	3♦	?

♠ A Q
♥ 5 4 2
♦ Q J 8 6 3
♣ J 5 4

East made a game try. Don't double. As on the previous hand, you have nothing to gain. You have everything to lose. Taking all your tricks is hard enough. Giving them away during the bidding makes it harder.

WEST	NORTH	EAST	SOUTH
1♥	Pass	3♥	Pass
4♣	Pass	4♦	?

♠ 8 5 4
♥ 8 7 6
♦ K Q 10 3
♣ 10 5 2

This time, a double is necessary. You are not going to be on lead. Your partner is. Help him out. If you don't double, they will end up in a heart contract. Your partner will think to himself that leading spades, the unbid suit, might be wise. Tell him you want a diamond lead. Admit it. Wouldn't you prefer to see him lead the ♦J than the ♠3?

POSTMORTEM

Unnecessary penalty doubles are costly. Kick the habit.

WHEN YOU'RE IN the middle of a bidding sequence, it's natural that you want to make as descriptive a bid as possible. Here is a very small quiz to show what I am talking about. Which of the following opening bids is most descriptive?

1♣   1♦   1♥   1♠   1NT

The answer is that a 1NT bid is fairly precise. 15–17 balanced points.

1♣, 1♦, 1♥, and 1♠ can show from eleven to twenty points and the shape can range from balanced to wildly distributional.

My suggestion is this. If you have a bid to make that isn't precise, consider bidding notrump instead. Examples make this easier to discuss.

WEST	NORTH	EAST	SOUTH
			?

♠ K Q
♥ J 5 4
♦ J 5 4
♣ A K Q 10 9

Bid 1NT. You show your points and shape. If you open 1♣, you can't tell partner you have sixteen balanced points.

WEST	NORTH	EAST	SOUTH
	1♦	Pass	1♥
Pass	1♠	Pass	?

♠ J
♥ K J 4 3
♦ 3 2
♣ Q J 9 8 6 5

Bid 1NT. This time you are more or less forced to do it because all other bids, including 2♣, show more strength.

WEST	NORTH	EAST	SOUTH
			1♦
Pass	1♥	Pass	?

♠ K 2
♥ K 2
♦ A J 8 5 3
♣ Q 7 5 3

You have two possible rebids. You can rebid 2♣, showing your second suit, or you can rebid 1NT. I suggest bidding 1NT. This bid tells partner almost everything about your hand. A 2♣ bid is vague. You can have 12–18 points with from 4-4 in the minors up to 6-5 in the minors when you rebid 2♣.

Does bidding notrump help responder? You bet it does. You are South and have:

♠ 9 2
♥ K 7 6 5 4 3
♦ Q 2
♣ K 9 5

The bidding starts:

WEST	NORTH	EAST	SOUTH
	1♦	Pass	1♥
Pass	2♣	Pass	?

You have to decide whether to pass, rebid 2♥, or even to take a preference to 2♦. Whatever you do runs the risk of being wrong. If your partner rebids 1NT, you have one pleasant choice. You can bid 2♥ knowing that your partner will almost always have two or three hearts.

QUICKIE

Be sure to alert properly. If you forget, you will be subject to penalty if the opponents can show they were hurt.

HAND
61

DO YOU KNOW why you overcall in a suit after your RHO opens with one of a suit?

How many reasons can you think of? (Note that jump overcalls and notrump overcalls are not covered here.)

In no particular order, the usual reasons I am given for making an overcall are:

1. Lead directing
2. Your side may own the hand.
3. Your overcall may disrupt the opponents' bidding.
4. You may find a good save.

Assuming you can't come up with another reason for over-calling, how would you rank these four reasons in terms of importance?

The important things are obstructing the opponents and bidding your hands accurately to your own contract when you own the hand. I rate the four reasons this way:

Bidding to your own contracts. .100
Obstructing the opponents. 90
Lead directing. 20
Finding a save. 8

There is one fact that surprises many players. Lead directing is way down the list.

Here's why. When you overcall, your LHO has to play the hand for lead direction to have any importance. Otherwise, you are on lead. More often than not, your LHO will either raise opener, make a negative double, or pass. Even if LHO bids a new suit, opener may rebid notrump. One way or the other, opener plays more hands than responder.

ON THE PREVIOUS hand, I stated that obstruction is one of the most important reasons for overcalling. Because the benefit is 'invisible' to the overcaller, you may not realize how much consternation you are causing the opponents. Let me show you.

♠ 6 4
♥ K Q 9 6 3
♦ K J 7
♣ 6 3 2

Your partner opens 1♣. You respond 1♥ and partner rebids 1NT showing 12–14 points. You pass and a simple auction is history. You know when you put your dummy down that your bidding has been reasonable.

Now note your comfort level when your RHO, instead of passing, overcalls 1♠ over partner's 1♣ bid. What should you do now? I'll let you mull over the problem. I predict that you won't be confident in your solution.

What was there about that 1♠ overcall that bugged you so? It bugged you because it deprived you of making your normal bid at the one level. You couldn't bid 1♥ anymore. Annoying. It's possible you won't reach your best contract.

Here is a list of the most annoying overcalls you can make, and a couple that aren't annoying:

1♣ – 1♠   Very annoying. Stops them from bidding 1♦ or 1♥.

1♦ – 1♠   Very annoying. Stops them from bidding 1♥.

1♦ – 2♣   Very annoying. Stops them from bidding 1♥ or 1♠ or 1NT. Be aggressive with this overcall. Your opponents won't appreciate it.

1♣ – 1♦ Not annoying at all.

1♣ – 1♥ A tiny bit annoying. Responder can't bid 1♦. That's all.

1♣	Pass	1♥	2♦
?			

1♦	Pass	1♥	2♣
?			

Both of these overcalls stop opener from rebidding 1♠.

This can be disturbing to opener when he has something like this hand:

♠ K Q 7 3
♥ K 4
♦ A Q 7 3
♣ 10 7 2

This hand opens 1♦, partner responds 1♥, and just as you are about to rebid 1♠, your RHO comes in with 2♣. Your choices are almost non-existent. You can pass and risk missing a 4-4 spade fit. Or you can rebid 2♠ and get too high when partner plays you for more. Rats.

HAND 63

IT IS NICE to have a lot of points. The more, the merrier. Sometimes, though, you don't get the dummy you wish for and you find yourself staring at a hopeless hand with only a stray queen or jack. The point of this very short article is to show you how a few little hands work opposite some strong hands.

You have the big hand below. Which dummy do you prefer?

DECLARER	DUMMY ONE
♠ A K 10 8 6 5 3	♠ 9 7 2
♥ K Q 6	♥ J 4
♦ –	♦ 10 8 6 5 3
♣ A K 4	♣ 7 5 2

DECLARER	DUMMY TWO
♠ A K 10 8 6 5 3	♠ 9
♥ K Q 6	♥ 9 5 4 2
♦ –	♦ K Q 10 2
♣ A K 4	♣ 9 5 3 2

The first dummy, with its solitary jack, will make 6♠ as long as spades are 2-1. The ♥J will let you set up a heart trick to discard dummy's small club. The three little spades will help draw trump.

The second dummy is worthless if the defense doesn't give declarer a diamond trick. If spades divide 3-2, game might still be down. If spades divide 4-1, it might be down two.

Here's another hand. If you are declarer, which dummy do you prefer? What contract would you like to be in?

DECLARER	DUMMY ONE
♠ A K 6 2	♠ Q 8
♥ 2	♥ 10 8 6
♦ A K 6 2	♦ 9 8 7 5 4 3
♣ A 9 7 3	♣ 8 5

DECLARER	DUMMY TWO
♠ A K 6 2	♠ Q 8 3
♥ 2	♥ A K J 5 3
♦ A K 6 2	♦ J 8 3
♣ A 9 7 3	♣ Q 8

The first of these two dummies will make 6♦ as long as trumps are 2-1. Declarer gets a lot of mileage out of his two-point dummy, which has the useful ♠Q and not the worthless ♣Q.

The second dummy offers lots of high cards. But if things don't break, there might not be a game.

What's the point of these two examples? The point is that high cards are not the only criterion for success. Winning contracts depend on a combination of the following:

1. High cards in the right places
2. Distribution
3. A fit

POSTMORTEM

Whatever high cards you have, whatever distribution you have, if they don't fit well, you may have nothing. On the two hands above, a one-point hand turned out to be more useful than a five-point hand. And a two-point hand turned out to be more useful than a thirteen-point hand. Things like this will happen. You should learn the symptoms.

Playing a hand is something that does not come easily. There are all kinds of guidelines you can use, but you have to pick the right guideline to use.

Take the issue of drawing trumps.

- Should you draw them immediately?
- Should you draw some of the trumps?
- Should you draw all of the trumps?
- Should you do some ruffing first?
- Should you use them to set up tricks in a side suit?
- Are you in danger of running out of trumps?

There are many things to consider when playing a hand.

In *Insights on Bridge—Book 2*, you will have a chance to play many hands that require a bit of thought. Rarely are you faced with a hand where you have nothing to think about. Normally, decisions have to be made. Many of these decisions have to be addressed at trick one. Some at trick twelve. You want to be sure not to make a decision before its time or after its time.

One thing I can say is that when you play a hand, you need to pay attention to the bidding and to the cards you see played. If at trick six you need to make a decision and you don't recall the facts, you will often be reduced to a guess when all the evidence was in front of you.

South Deals + No One Vulnerable

♠ K Q 8 5 2
♥ 8 4
♦ 9 4 3
♣ A 6 4

♠ 4 3
♥ A K Q J 10 6
♦ A 5
♣ 9 7 2

WEST	NORTH	EAST	SOUTH
			1♥
Dbl	1♠	Pass	3♥
Pass	4♥	All pass	

SOUTH BIDS 1♥ and West doubles. North gives no thought to redoubling. It's almost always better to make a natural bid than to redouble. 1♠ is forcing, so North will get another chance. South, with seven sure winners, jumps to 3♥, and North continues to game. Note that North, with two little hearts, raises hearts instead of rebidding spades. Opposite a jump rebid, 84 is adequate support.

West leads the ♦K.

West's lead is good for South. A club lead would have hurt since it would attack the club entry that South will need later. South's plan must be to set up two spade tricks to go with the eight top tricks already available. How should South play?

There is a danger here. If you draw trump and lead spades, West will duck the first spade. You won't be able to come back to your hand to lead a second spade. The way to get around this is to win the ♦A. Take just one round of trumps and lead a spade. Assuming West ducks, you will come to your hand with a trump and draw as many more trumps as necessary. Now you lead your second spade. West will take it, but your club entry is still there to get to the spade trick. Nice forethought.

The layout:

<pre>
                    ♠ K Q 8 5 2
                    ♥ 8 4
                    ♦ 9 4 3
                    ♣ A 6 4

      ♠ A J 9 7   ♠ 10 6
      ♥ 3   ♥ 9 7 5 2
      ♦ K Q 10 6   ♦ J 8 7 2
      ♣ Q J 5 3   ♣ K 10 8

                    ♠ 4 3
                    ♥ A K Q J 10 6
                    ♦ A 5
                    ♣ 9 7 2
</pre>

POSTMORTEM

Entries are one of the most important tools a declarer or a defender has. Players often abuse them by taking them prematurely.

Here's a simple suit combination. Any suit will do.

♥ A K Q

♥ 4 3 2

To some players, this combination represents three easy tricks. To someone who knows about entries, he will recognize that if he wishes to do so, he can get to dummy three times using the cards above.

♠ 7 6 2
♥ 7 3
♦ A K 9 2
♣ 7 6 5 2

♠ A K Q
♥ A 9
♦ Q 7 5 4 3
♣ A 8 4

WEST	NORTH	EAST	SOUTH
			1♦
Pass	2♦	Pass	?

SOUTH SHOULD BID 3NT. He will bid 3NT with most of his nineteen-point hands, as well as some slightly weaker hands that have longer diamonds to use as tricks.

West leads the ♥Q.

South has eight top tricks, and ten if the diamonds behave. After winning the ♥A, what should South do next?

South must make a thoughtful play. He is going to play on diamonds. If South is accustomed to bad luck, he will consider what can stop him from running diamonds. On this hand, it's a good idea.

Here is the complete hand:

```
                 ♠  7 6 2
                 ♥  7 3
                 ♦  A K 9 2
                 ♣  7 6 5 2

   ♠ 10 8 3                      ♠  J 9 5 4
   ♥ Q J 10 2                    ♥  K 8 6 5 4
   ♦ J 10 8 6                    ♦  –
   ♣ K J                         ♣  Q 10 9 3

                 ♠  A K Q
                 ♥  A 9
                 ♦  Q 7 5 4 3
                 ♣  A 8 4
```

On this layout West has all the diamonds. It is a rare event but it is one that can be catered to. South must play the ♦Q, which will give him the news about the bad break in time to use it. He can later lead toward dummy and finesse West out of his diamonds.

This is not a difficult hand as long as you spend a little time thinking before dashing into the play. With experience, you will learn to think about possible bad luck and then to look for a solution. Well done if you do the right thing on hands like this one.

South Deals   +   Both Sides Vulnerable

♠ Q J 7 3
♥ K Q 6
♦ A 8
♣ Q 10 4 2

♠ A 6 5 2
♥ 8 3 2
♦ K 10
♣ A K J 6

WEST	NORTH	EAST	SOUTH
			1NT
Pass	2♣	Pass	2♠
Pass	4♠	All pass	

SITTING SOUTH, YOU have enough for a 1NT opening bid. North asks for a major and you show your spades. A second later you are in game. West leads the ♥J and North puts down a considerably good hand, commenting as he does so, "Wonder if I should have looked for slam."

A preliminary look at the hand shows that your side has duplicated distribution, almost always a bad sign. It means you can't get any ruffing tricks and you won't have any discards either.

You put up a heart honor from dummy and East wins the trick, as expected. Back comes a heart, which you win in dummy. This is a bad start. South now addresses the trump suit. This is a layout that you have seen before and will see again. How do you play?

Carefully. If spades are 4-1, leading the queen for a finesse will lose two tricks no matter how they are distributed. Here's the layout that you are worried about:

```
              ♠  Q J 7 3
              ♥  K Q 6
              ♦  A 8
              ♣  Q 10 4 2

♠  K 10 9 8                      ♠  4
♥  J 10 9 7                      ♥  A 5 4
♦  Q 7 3                         ♦  J 9 6 5 4 2
♣  9 7                          ♣  8 5 3

              ♠  A 6 5 2
              ♥  8 3 2
              ♦  K 10
              ♣  A K J 6
```

You can see that leading the queen will leave you with two losers in spades. The proper play with this trump suit is to lead to the ace and back towards the QJxx. If East has K10xx, you are down no matter what. Bad luck. But if West has K10xx, you can hold him to one trick. It's possible that you will drop someone's singleton king.

This suit combination is one of many that you need to become familiar with.

♠ K J 7 6
♥ K 9 5
♦ J 9 7
♣ 8 7 4

♠ A Q 10 4 2
♥ A 7 4
♦ Q 6 2
♣ J 5

WEST	NORTH	EAST	SOUTH
			1♠
Pass	Pass	Pass	1♠
Pass	2♠	All pass	

WEST LED THE ♣K and continued with a club to East's ace and a third club, ruffed by South. Since South could afford it, he ruffed with an honor. Next, South drew trump, which divided two-two.

At this point, South has two diamond losers and a heart loser, and is in danger of losing three diamonds. If West has the ♦10, South can make 2♠ by finessing the nine. Is this the best play and if not, what is?

Hint: Endplay.

This hand lends itself to using an endplay. Do you see it?

After drawing trumps, South plays three rounds of hearts. Whichever defender wins this trick, he will have to do something to help South. If the defender leads diamonds, the defense will get two tricks. If the defense leads a heart or a club, giving South a sluff and a ruff, he discards a diamond and loses the same two diamond tricks.

Here is the complete hand:

                        ♠ K J 7 6
                        ♥ K 9 5
                        ♦ J 9 7
                        ♣ 8 7 4

    ♠ 8 5   ♠ 9 3
    ♥ Q 10 8   ♥ J 6 3 2
    ♦ K 8 5 3   ♦ A 10 4
    ♣ K Q 9 2   ♣ A 10 6 3

                        ♠ A Q 10 4 2
                        ♥ A 7 4
                        ♦ Q 6 2
                        ♣ J 5

POSTMORTEM

Some hands do not require you do much thinking. This is one
of them. Once South ruffs the third club and finds trumps divide evenly, the hand is cold. No matter what the layout, the
endplay works just fine.

East Deals + North-South Vulnerable

♠ 10 9 3
♥ J 6 4
♦ A Q J 3
♣ J 10 4

♠ A K Q 8 4 2
♥ Q 7
♦ 7 2
♣ A Q 9

WEST	NORTH	EAST	SOUTH
		1♥	1♠
Pass	2♠	3♥	4♠
All pass			

SOUTH OVERCALLED 1♠ with a very nice hand. North made a modest raise to 2♠ and South went to game. All reasonable.

West leads the ♥8 and East takes his king and ace, West following on the second trick with the ♥3. Back comes a third heart. How should South play here?

What South did was ruff the heart with the ♠Q, keeping West from getting a heart ruff. This was expensive.

South next played the ♠A and king, which showed that West had started with the ♠J65. West now has a spade winner. With a spade loser still to come for the defense, South had to rely on both minor suit finesses. The club finesse worked, predictably, but the diamond finesse lost, also predictably.

South ended up with nine tricks.

Given the bidding, how should South do better?

South made an error by fighting over the third trick. When he ruffed, he set up a spade trick for the defense and he kept a diamond loser.

If South goes quietly, he will discard a diamond on the heart. West gets his ruff but because South has only one diamond remaining, he has no losers there. He still has to take a club finesse but on the bidding, that is practically assured.

The complete hand:

```
               ♠  10 9 3
               ♥  J 6 4
               ♦  A Q J 3
               ♣  J 10 4

♠  J 6 5                        ♠  7
♥  8 3                          ♥  A K 10 9 5 2
♦  9 8 5 4                      ♦  K 10 6
♣  8 6 5 2                      ♣  K 7 3

               ♠  A K Q 8 4 2
               ♥  Q 7
               ♦  7 2
               ♣  A Q 9
```

POSTMORTEM

Is there a way to bid to 3NT or is that thought a postmortem fantasy?

West Deals + No One Vulnerable

♠ A K J
♥ 2
♦ Q 10 7 6 3
♣ K J 8 2

♠ 10 9 8 7 6 3
♥ A 6 5 3
♦ A
♣ 9 3

WEST	NORTH	EAST	SOUTH
3♥	Dbl	Pass	4♠
All pass			

4♠ ENDS THE bidding. West gets off to the lead of the ♥K, East following with the jack. How should South play to take ten tricks?

South blew it at trick two.

South got busy ruffing hearts in dummy. There was bad news, however, when East overruffed the ♠J with the queen. East returned a trump. After this start South was able to ruff one heart in dummy, but that left South with a heart loser and two club losers when East had the ace and queen.

Unlucky? Yes. Preventable? Yes.

South didn't listen to the bidding. Given that East rated to have one heart, South should have ruffed a heart with the ♠A. Return to his hand with the ♦A and ruff a heart with the ♠K. Back to his hand with a diamond ruff and ruff his last heart with the ♠J. This is one trick that South does not mind having over-ruffed because South has no more hearts to ruff in dummy. In the fullness of time East gets two club tricks, but South has the rest of the tricks with his good spade spots.

$$\spadesuit \text{ A K J}$$
$$\heartsuit \text{ 2}$$
$$\diamondsuit \text{ Q 10 7 6 3}$$
$$\clubsuit \text{ K J 8 2}$$

$$\spadesuit \text{ 5} \qquad\qquad \spadesuit \text{ Q 4 2}$$
$$\heartsuit \text{ K Q 10 9 8 7 4} \qquad \heartsuit \text{ J}$$
$$\diamondsuit \text{ 5 4} \qquad\qquad \diamondsuit \text{ K J 9 8 2}$$
$$\clubsuit \text{ 6 5 4} \qquad\qquad \clubsuit \text{ A Q 10 7}$$

$$\spadesuit \text{ 10 9 8 7 6 3}$$
$$\heartsuit \text{ A 6 5 3}$$
$$\diamondsuit \text{ A}$$
$$\clubsuit \text{ 9 3}$$

POSTMORTEM

Do you agree with South's 4♠ bid?

South did well in the bidding. Look at the North hand. If South had bid 3♠, North would rate his hand as being worth around 15 points. Having only three spades is poor given that his double implies three or more. North barely has his double and would have passed 3♠. Fortunately, South evaluated his hand accurately and game was efficiently bid. And ought to have been made.

HAND 70

♠ 7
♥ K 10 5
♦ Q J 8 7 4 2
♣ A 4 3

♠ A K 6 2
♥ A Q J 9 3
♦ 9 6
♣ J 9

WEST	NORTH	EAST	SOUTH
			1♥
Pass	1NT	Pass	2♣
Pass	3♥	Pass	4♥
All pass			

THE BIDDING INCLUDES a quirk of the Two Over One system. When North makes a forcing 1NT response, South has to bid his two-card club suit. He can't reverse to 2♠ and he can't rebid his hearts. That promises six. 2♣ is the answer. Only if he gets passed out in 2♣ and if partner has four clubs, will South be really unhappy. Bidding 2♣ will be safe most of the time. North jumped to 3♥ showing a three-card limit raise, and South went to game.

West leads a heart. South might start ruffing spades, but that's not going to work. At most, South will get one spade ruff in dummy. He needs two.

When faced with a hand like this one, declarer should always think of the merit of using a suit in dummy rather than trying to get ruffs in dummy. Here's the layout. You need a little luck, but not a lot.

```
                    ♠  7
                    ♥  K 10 5
                    ♦  Q J 8 7 4 2
                    ♣  A 4 3

    ♠  Q 10 8 4                    ♠  J 9 5 3
    ♥  8 4                         ♥  7 6 2
    ♦  K 10 3                      ♦  A 5
    ♣  Q 8 5 2                     ♣  K 10 7 6

                    ♠  A K 6 2
                    ♥  A Q J 9 3
                    ♦  9 6
                    ♣  J 9
```

Starting diamonds at trick two is best. In order to do that, South wins the first trick in his hand, not in the dummy.

East will win the first diamond. He will return a heart, won by South. Declarer will play another diamond and West will take his king.

At this point South can draw trump and claim since the diamonds are good and there is an entry to dummy.

POSTMORTEM

Ruffing something in dummy may feel like getting tricks for free. But there are other ways to win tricks than by ruffing.

When East wins his ♦A, he can switch to a club away from his king. This will get the defenders one more trick.

South Deals   +   No One Vulnerable

♠ K 8 6 5
♥ A J 3
♦ Q 3
♣ A 10 6 2

♠ 9 7 2
♥ K 10 4
♦ A K 8 5
♣ K 8 5

WEST	NORTH	EAST	SOUTH
			1♦
Pass	1♠	Pass	1NT
Pass	3NT	All pass	

AFTER A SIMPLE value auction, you arrive in 3NT. West leads the ♥2. East plays the nine and you win with the ten. You have two ways to get a ninth trick. You can play for a spade trick or for an extra club trick. What is your best chance?

```
                    ♠ K 8 6 5
                    ♥ A J 3
                    ♦ Q 3
                    ♣ A 10 6 2

♠ Q 3                                       ♠ A J 10 4
♥ Q 8 7 2                                   ♥ 9 6 5
♦ 10 7 6 4 2                                ♦ J 9
♣ Q 4                                       ♣ J 9 7 3

                    ♠ 9 7 2
                    ♥ K 10 4
                    ♦ A K 8 5
                    ♣ K 8 5
```

Try taking some spade finesses. Don't lead to the ♠K. Instead, lead the ♠9 and if West doesn't cover, let it ride. East will win the ten. Win the heart return, as good a play for East as there is, and lead the ♠7. West will cover with the queen, dummy covers with the king, and East gets his ace. If you have been paying attention to the spade spots, dummy's eight and six are strong enough to knock out the opponents' remaining spade honor. You win the heart return and lead another spade. East takes his jack, but even if East has the thirteenth heart to take, you still have nine winners. East's remaining spade is the four. Whatever spade North has left is good.

POSTMORTEM

Note that if you'd started clubs you wouldn't succeed, and now you won't be able to bring in a spade trick.

This is an interesting hand in that every one of the spade spots is needed. If East had the seven or the eight, the play used here wouldn't work.

West Deals   +   No One Vulnerable

♠ J 4 3
♥ A 6 3
♦ K 10 6 4
♣ 9 4 3

♠ Q
♥ 9 5 4
♦ Q J 3
♣ K Q J 8 7 6

WEST	NORTH	EAST	SOUTH
1♠	Pass	3♠*	4♣
4♠	5♣	Dbl	All pass

*LIMIT

TRYING TO HELP North out on opening lead, South bid 4♣
over East's limit raise. West continued to 4♠, and North went
on to 5♣. East doubled, and that was that. Not a triumph for
North-South.

West leads the ♠6 to East's ace. How should South continue
when East returns a spade?

```
              ♠ J 4 3
              ♥ A 6 3
              ♦ K 10 6 4
              ♣ 9 4 3

♠ K 10 8 6 5                    ♠ A 9 7 2
♥ Q 10 8                        ♥ K J 7 2
♦ A 9                           ♦ 8 7 5 2
♣ A 10 5                        ♣ 2

              ♠ Q
              ♥ 9 5 4
              ♦ Q J 3
              ♣ K Q J 8 7 6
```

This is the kind of play you should spot immediately. It is called the loser on loser play. Instead of ruffing the spade return, discard one of your two heart losers. West will win the spade and will probably switch to hearts as fast as he can. But it will be too late. Declarer is in control. South grabs the ♥A, discards his other heart on the ♠J, and proceeds to draw trumps. His only losers are two spades and two aces.

Note how badly the defenders played. East knew declarer was out of spades and would use the loser on loser play if needed. East might not have wanted to lead a heart back, but leading a spade back was awful. Had East not returned a spade, the defenders would have gotten one more trick than they did. On this hand, the trick the defenders lost was a doubled undertrick. Expensive stuff.

POSTMORTEM

You should recognize this position as a defender so as not to give declarer a free trick. And you should recognize this position when you declare so you can take advantage if given the chance.

South Deals   +   East-West Vulnerable

♠ A K 7 6 5 2
♥ 6 5 3
♦ 8 7
♣ 8 5

♠ 3
♥ A K Q 4
♦ A Q
♣ A K Q J 10 6

WEST	NORTH	EAST	SOUTH
			2♣
Pass	2♠	Pass	3♣
Pass	3♠	Pass	4NT
Pass	5♥	Pass	7NT
All pass			

SOUTH HAS ONE of the best hands you will ever see. He starts with a strong 2♣ and then shows his clubs while North bids spades twice. Over 3♠, South more or less has to bid Blackwood, which tells him that North has the ♠AK. The final bid is mildly chancy, but since 7NT will be no worse than a diamond finesse, South tries for the maximum.

West leads the ♠Q.

This is an easy problem although it comes with emotional connotations. South starts by taking dummy's two spade winners and must decide what to discard from his hand. Should South discard the ♦Q and rely on a 3-3 heart split, or should he discard the little heart and rely on the diamond finesse? While you are mulling this over, recognize that if you take the diamond finesse, you have to do so right now. If it loses, West may cash some spade tricks. If you play for 3-3 hearts, you will make or be down one.

```
                    ♠  A K 7 6 5 2
                    ♥  6 5 3
                    ♦  8 7
                    ♣  8 5

   ♠  Q J 10 9                          ♠  8 4
   ♥  9 7                               ♥  J 10 8 2
   ♦  10 9 6 5 3 2                      ♦  K J 4
   ♣  2                                 ♣  9 7 4 3

                    ♠  3
                    ♥  A K Q 4
                    ♦  A Q
                    ♣  A K Q J 10 6
```

It helps to know some common percentages. The diamond finesse is a 50% chance and the hearts dividing 3-3 is about 35%. The odds are in favor of the diamond finesse.

POSTMORTEM

Do you think that South should bid the grand slam? Hard to say. I point out that if West had led a diamond, the slam would be cold. And, if West leads a club or a heart, declarer will be able to take the three top hearts first and then take the diamond finesse later if needed. 7NT is an OK spot.

South Deals　+　No One Vulnerable

♠ Q J 7 5
♥ 7 6 5 2
♦ J 4
♣ 8 7 2

♠ A K 10 4
♥ Q 8 4
♦ A K 5
♣ A K J

WEST	NORTH	EAST	SOUTH
			2♣
Pass	2♦	Pass	2NT
Pass	3♣	Pass	3♠
Pass	4♠	All pass	

NORTH-SOUTH HAVE a sensible sequence to 4♠. South has too much to open 2NT so he opens 2♣ instead. North has a poor hand and responds 2♦. North could have a good hand with no convenient bid, but for now, South will expect a poor one. South's 2NT rebid shows 22–24 points, so North just barely has enough to ask for a major and go to game.

West leads the ♥A and switches to the ♠9. South wins the spade lead and draws a second round, seeing that they divide 3-2. South can finish drawing trump and ruff a diamond. A winning club finesse will do the job. Can it be avoided?

Maybe.

Instead of ruffing diamonds or finessing clubs, South should lead a heart. If a heart trick can be set up for a club discard, the club finesse will be unnecessary. Here's the layout:

```
              ♠ Q J 7 5
              ♥ 7 6 5 2
              ♦ J 4
              ♣ 8 7 2

♠ 9 8 3                        ♠ 6 2
♥ A K J                        ♥ 10 9 3
♦ 8 7 6 2                      ♦ Q 10 9 3
♣ Q 9 5                        ♣ 10 6 4 3

              ♠ A K 10 4
              ♥ Q 8 4
              ♦ A K 5
              ♣ A K J
```

The club finesse will lose, but it's not necessary. The extra chance of 3-3 hearts comes home.

POSTMORTEM

Finesses are a staple of good dummy play but sometimes they can wait. Sometime they can be avoided all together.

South Deals   +   No One Vulnerable

♠ K 10 2
♥ A Q 7 3
♦ 5 3
♣ K 9 5 2

♠ 8 7 3
♥ K J 9 8 6 4
♦ A Q
♣ A 3

WEST	NORTH	EAST	SOUTH
			1♥
1♠	2♠	Pass	4♥
All pass			

SOUTH OPENS 1♥ and West puts in a 1♠ overcall. North's 2♠ cuebid shows a balanced game-forcing heart raise. If North had eleven points he would make a limit raise to 3♥, which South could pass. As science goes, this treatment is reasonable because it lets North show the kind of hand he has right away.

West leads the ♠Q. Your plan?

```
              ♠ K 10 2
              ♥ A Q 7 3
              ♦ 5 3
              ♣ K 9 5 2

   ♠ Q J 9 6 5              ♠ A 4
   ♥ 5                      ♥ 10 2
   ♦ K J 7 4                ♦ 10 9 8 6 2
   ♣ Q J 4                  ♣ 10 8 7 6

              ♠ 8 7 3
              ♥ K J 9 8 6 4
              ♦ A Q
              ♣ A 3
```

Unless you are a suspicious player, you should not cover the ♠Q. Do you see why?

True, covering assures you will get a spade trick, but not covering should also get you a spade trick. You know West has the ♠J so you can finesse the ten later. Why not cover the queen on the first trick?

It all goes back to the bidding. If you noticed West's 1♠ bid, you can imagine that he has five of them. If you cover, East will win the ace and return his second spade. West will win and give East a spade ruff. A later diamond loser will set 4♥ one trick.

POSTMORTEM

Note the small bonus that comes from ducking the spade lead. East might have had the singleton ace. If so, ducking will hold your spade losers to just one.

North Deals + North-South Vulnerable

♠ 10 7 6 4 3 2
♥ 10 7
♦ 3
♣ A 8 6 3

♠ A K 9 5
♥ J 5
♦ A K J 10
♣ 5 4 2

WEST	NORTH	EAST	SOUTH
	Pass	Pass	1NT
Pass	2♥*	Dbl	3♠
Pass	4♠	All pass	

*TRANSFER

SOUTH OPENED 1NT and North bid 2♥, a transfer to spades. East doubled 2♥. Both North and South were a little bit aggressive, and South ended up in 4♠. West leads the ♥3. East takes the ♥K and ace and switches to the ♣Q. Declarer wins and draws trumps in two rounds, West having the singleton ♠Q and East the ♠J8.

There is still the little problem of two club losers. You can finesse East for the ♦Q, which will give you two discards from dummy. Or you can play the ace and king and then lead the jack for a trump finesse against West.

If you can guess where the ♦Q is, you will make 4♠. Where is it?

You should know where it is by now. Count the high cards you have seen. Then review the bidding. East passed and has shown up with the ♠J, the ♥AK, and the ♣Q. That adds up to ten points. You suspect that East also has the ♣J. That would give him eleven points. If East had the ♦Q, he would have opened the bidding. West has it. Play the ♦A and king and lead the jack. If West covers, you ruff and later discard another club from dummy. If West does not cover, discard the club and hope your card-reading was correct.

♠ 10 7 6 4 3 2
♥ 10 7
♦ 3
♣ A 8 6 3

♠ Q	♠ J 8
♥ Q 9 6 3	♥ A K 8 4 2
♦ Q 8 6 5 2	♦ 9 7 4
♣ K 9 7	♣ Q J 10

♠ A K 9 5
♥ J 5
♦ A K J 10
♣ 5 4 2

POSTMORTEM

In the bidding, South jumped to 3♠ instead of bidding 2♠. This jump shows:

- A useful maximum 1NT
- Four or more spades
- Good shape

South is in the ballpark. He would not jump to 3♠ if he had 4-3-3-3 distribution.

South Deals   +   Both Sides Vulnerable

♠ 4
♥ K Q 5 3
♦ A K 10 9 7 6
♣ K 3

♠ Q J 9 6 3
♥ A J 10 8 4
♦ Q J
♣ A

WEST	NORTH	EAST	SOUTH
			1♠
Pass	2♦	Pass	2♥
Pass	4NT	Pass	5♥
Pass	6♥	All pass	

HANDS WITH DISTRIBUTION are nice to look at, but until a fit is found they may not be so nice to hold. Here, good things happen immediately. South bids 1♠ and North responds 2♦. With the ♦QJ, South's hand is already showing signs of getting better. South's 2♥ bid catches an enthusiastic response from North. After Blackwooding, North signs off in 6♥. How should you play when West leads the ♠A, then the five?

Careful does it. Why in the world is West defending this way? One would have expected a club lead against 6♥. Do you see any problem? Can you do something about it?

The answer is that the optimist ruffs in dummy and starts to claim, stating that he is drawing trumps and running diamonds. The pessimist also ruffs in dummy, but he is careful to ruff with the ♥K or queen. It's free to ruff high. With the top five hearts, it is safe to ruff with an honor because you still have the certainty that you can draw trumps. Here's the layout:

```
                    ♠  4
                    ♥  K Q 5 3
                    ♦  A K 10 9 7 6
                    ♣  K 3

    ♠ A K 10 8 7 5              ♠  2
    ♥ –                        ♥  9 7 6 2
    ♦ 8 3                      ♦  5 4 2
    ♣ J 9 7 6 2                ♣  Q 10 8 5 4

                    ♠  Q J 9 6 3
                    ♥  A J 10 8 4
                    ♦  Q J
                    ♣  A
```

POSTMORTEM

West made an intelligent lead that could have worked if East had something like the ♥10985.

South Deals   +   North-South Vulnerable

♠ A Q 7 3 2
♥ 6 4 3
♦ 7 6 3
♣ 6 5

♠ J 6 4
♥ A Q 10 5
♦ A Q 2
♣ J 9 8

WEST	NORTH	EAST	SOUTH
			1♣
Pass	1♠	Pass	1NT
All pass			

THE SEQUENCE TO 1NT is normal enough. North reasonably does not rebid spades.

West led the ♣4 into South's bid suit and struck gold when East produced the ♣A and queen and three. Ultimately, West showed up with five clubs, meaning you have to find three discards from the dummy. What do you discard and what is your plan?

Your best chance is to take spade tricks. You need to keep all five spades in the dummy and all three spades in your hand. On the last three clubs, discard three red cards from dummy, say two diamonds and one heart. East discards a small heart and a small diamond. When West finishes the clubs, he exits with the ♦5 to East's king and your ace. That's one trick in the bank for you. Now to the spades. When you lead the ♠4 toward dummy, West plays the king. Do you or don't you?

```
                    ♠  A Q 7 3 2
                    ♥  6 4 3
                    ♦  7 6 3
                    ♣  6 5

    ♠  K                         ♠  10 9 8 5
    ♥  K 8 7                     ♥  J 9 2
    ♦  J 10 8 5                  ♦  K 9 4
    ♣  K 10 7 4 2               ♣  A Q 3

                    ♠  J 6 4
                    ♥  A Q 10 5
                    ♦  A Q 2
                    ♣  J 9 8
```

If you want to assure that you make 1NT, you will let West have the ♠K. He continues with the ♦J to your queen. You now have four spades, two diamonds, and a heart. You can take the heart finesse at your own risk.

POSTMORTEM

RULE: When you are in a contract that doesn't look very exciting, you may need to force yourself to pay attention. Just because you are in a partscore doesn't mean the stakes are not worth fighting for.

Incidentally, if West doesn't play the ♠K, you will finesse dummy's queen. If that wins, you will continue with a small spade from dummy, hoping spades are 3-2.

If a hand looks easy, think if there is anything that can go wrong and if you can allow for it. An example:

♠ Q 6 4 2

♠ A K 9 7 3

This suit looks like five sure tricks. But...If the suit divides 4-0, there could be problems. Play the queen first. If your RHO has ♠J1085, you can pick them up. If LHO has ♠J1085, it was never to be. Think what bad can happen and look to see if you can compensate for it.

If you didn't ask what might go wrong, it is more likely to haunt you than if you ask.

Warning: Defense is tougher than declarer play. When you play a hand, you know what you and your dummy have as soon as the dummy comes down. When you are defending, you can see your hand and dummy but you don't know what partner has. You learn this one card at a time.

Some defensive hands are clear. Others are not. The defensive hands in *Insights on Bridge—Book 2* and later books in this series will offer a range of things to think about. Time and repetition will help.

BRIEF REVIEW OF LEADS AND SIGNALS

In this book, the signals used are normal. If you like something, you play a high card to encourage and a low card to discourage. On defense, you may give count signals. High-low shows an even number of cards and low-high shows an odd number of cards.

Leads are also normal.

Ace from AKx(x) against a suit.

King from KQx(x) against a suit.

There are a couple of interesting items to mention here. In general:

If you lead an ace against a suit contract, you promise the king. Partner will signal that he likes the suit if he has the queen or if he wants a ruff.

If you lead a king against a suit contract, you promise the queen and deny the ace. Partner will signal that he likes the suit if he has the jack or the ace. He may choose to play high-low if he thinks a ruff is possible. There's always a little ambiguity here.

When you play a hand, you need to remember the bidding and you need to pay attention to how the play has gone. If you forget to do either, you will end up making guesses instead of educated plays.

When you are defending, you need to do the same things. Here are two important habits you need to learn to follow when you see the dummy.

Habit One: Look at dummy's cards in the suit that was led. Be careful to note the spot cards. If declarer calls for a 'low' card from dummy, be sure you notice if it is a five or a two. This is your one and only chance to 'see' that card. It may be important soon. It may be important later.

Habit Two: On some auctions you will know immediately how many points your partner has. If declarer has opened 1NT showing 15–17 points, you should, when you see the dummy, work out how many points your partner has. This one is easy to do.

WHY YOU NEED TO KNOW
WHAT YOUR PARTNER IS DOING

You must know what your partner is telling you. You are on lead against 4♥ and you lead the ♠A from AK7. Dummy has the 6543. Your partner plays the two. I have already suggested that the two should say he doesn't like this suit. (But some players have other ideas.)

Is your partner discouraging?
Is your partner giving count?
Is your partner asking you to switch to a club?

Here's another common situation that needs partnership understandings. Say your partner plays the queen instead of the two. His queen says your partner has the jack, or perhaps a singleton queen.

What should you do?

Should you lead the king and another?
Should you lead low to partner's jack?
Should you switch to a heart?

The easy answer is that you have to decide what to do next. Partner is not giving you instructions. He is giving you information.

A promise: You cannot play that a card means one thing today and another thing tomorrow and a third thing next week.

I suggest you reread any of these hands that you are not sure of. Repetition is important. You don't practice golf by hitting putts for two minutes. The same with bridge.

Bon voyage.

QUICKIE

Pay attention! If someone were to ask you at trick five what the bidding was and the exact card that was led, you should know. Keep track of everything that happens. You can never tell when it is going to become important. Have you ever spent a minute at trick twelve wondering which card to keep? If you had paid attention, you would know. Fact: You can't remember something you didn't see or didn't hear.

East Deals + East-West Vulnerable

WEST	NORTH	EAST	SOUTH
		1♦	1♠
Pass	4♠	5♣	5♠
All pass			

NORTH
♠ K 8 6 4 2
♥ K
♦ Q 10 6 4
♣ 6 4 2

EAST
♠ 7
♥ 8 4
♦ A K 9 8 2
♣ A K Q 10 9

THIS HAND SHOWS a simple theme that can cause confusion. West leads the ♣J against South's 5♠. You overtake and cash another club, West following with the eight. In the meantime, declarer follows with the five and seven. All of this leaves the ♣3 still outstanding. Do you continue with a high club or do you cash the ♦A? Why?

Here is the complete hand:

```
              ♠ K 8 6 4 2
              ♥ K
              ♦ Q 10 6 4
              ♣ 6 4 2

♠ 9 3                          ♠ 7
♥ 9 7 6 5 3                    ♥ 8 4
♦ J 7 5 3                      ♦ A K 9 8 2
♣ J 8                          ♣ A K Q 10 9

              ♠ A Q J 10 5
              ♥ A Q J 10 2
              ♦ –
              ♣ 7 5 3
```

As you can see, it is necessary to cash the club. Note that if South had a small diamond and two clubs, it would have been necessary to cash a diamond. Declarer would have discarded dummy's diamonds on his hearts and would make 5♠. This situation is typical of many defensive problems where the solution depends on your knowledge of how partner will lead with various holdings.

Eddie Kantar offered the bridge world a useful guideline. You are on lead with three little cards in one of partner's suits.

If your partner bid a suit and you didn't raise him, lead low if you have three of them. Partner will know you don't have a doubleton.

If your partner bid a suit and you raised it and then lead it, lead a high one. Partner knows you have length in the suit. He can tell from your high card that you don't have an honor.

Is this guideline perfect? No, it's not. But it makes many hands easier than without it.

There are other reasons why leading a ten or nine from three cards such as 1083 or 964 isn't best. These layouts shows why. Say your partner has bid spades and you are leading against a notrump contract.

If you lead the ♠10, the play will continue with the queen from dummy, partner's king, and South's ace. East will get a later trick with the jack, but South's nine will be a winner. If West leads the three, South will not get a second winner in the suit.

If West leads the ♠9, East will know West doesn't have an honor in the suit. But when South wins a trick with the eight, East may decide that this information wasn't worth much.

Both of these disasters could have been avoided if West had led his lowest card.

North Deals   +   No One Vulnerable

WEST	NORTH	EAST	SOUTH
	1♣	Pass	1♥
Pass	2♥	Pass	4♥
All pass			

NORTH
♠ 8 3 2
♥ K Q 10 5
♦ A 5
♣ K J 8 2

WEST
♠ A K 7 4
♥ 8 7 3
♦ K 9 3
♣ 5 4 3

You lead the ♠A.

Case One. Partner plays the ♠5. What does it mean? What do you do?

Partner's play is discouraging. The ♠5 is the smallest outstanding spade. He is denying the queen. He is saying he sees no future in your leading another spade. He is not saying he wants you to lead another suit. He is just saying that from his perspective, another spade isn't best. If you know a spade continuation is best, do so.

Importantly, *he is not telling you to lead a club.*

Case Two. Partner plays the ♠9. What does it mean? What do you do?

This is a high spot and it says he likes spades. He may have the queen. He may have a doubleton. In either case, you should continue with the king and a small one.

Case Three. Partner plays the ♠Q. This is a very important moment in the defense. Do you know what it means? Are you sure?

He is saying that he has the jack too. He is telling you that you can continue with the king or if you wish, you can lead a small spade to his jack.

Many players think that the queen says West must lead to East's jack. This is a big error. East is informing West that East has the jack. West has the option of leading to East's jack. West does not have to do that. West does whatever he thinks is best.

Here's a possible hand:

```
              ♠  8 3 2
              ♥  K Q 10 5
              ♦  A 5
              ♣  K J 8 2

♠  A K 7 4                      ♠  Q J 9
♥  8 7 3                        ♥  2
♦  K 9 3                        ♦  10 8 7 6 4 2
♣  5 4 3                        ♣  Q 7 6

              ♠  10 6 5
              ♥  A J 9 6 4
              ♦  Q J
              ♣  A 10 9
```

Let's say that West leads to East's ♠J. East will continue with his ♠9, which West will win. West will see that there is no reason to lead a club or a diamond and he will make a safe lead of a heart. This concept of doing 'nothing' is important.

A defender does not have to find a killing play every time he makes a play. Making safe plays is just as important as being dynamic. When West leads a heart at trick four, declarer is forced to guess where the ♣Q is if he is to make 4♥. Perhaps he will. Perhaps he won't. If West leads a club at trick four, South won't have to guess where the queen is. The defenders will have located it for him.

West Deals + North-South Vulnerable

WEST	NORTH	EAST	SOUTH
1♦	2♣	Pass	2♠
3♦	3♠	Pass	4♠
All pass			

NORTH
♠ 6 4 2
♥ A 8
♦ Q J 9
♣ A K J 10 7

WEST
♠ A 7
♥ 10 5 4
♦ A K 8 7 6 5 4
♣ 8

YOU LEAD THE ♦A, getting the two from partner and the three from declarer. The ten is missing. Is 4♠ beatable or should you hope to hold it to four?

You should beat this. It's almost 100% to go down if your side does everything right. What is the key to the defense?

The key is partner's ♦2. In a situation like this, your partner is obliged to give you a count signal. The missing diamond is the ten. If partner had it, he would play it to show you a doubleton.

This means declarer has the ten. Rather than cash your ♦K, you should switch to the ♣8. When you get in with the ♠A, you will lead a low diamond for partner to ruff. You will get a club ruff in return for down one.

Here's the layout:

```
              ♠ 6 4 2
              ♥ A 8
              ♦ Q J 9
              ♣ A K J 10 7

♠ A 7                          ♠ 10 8
♥ 10 5 4                       ♥ Q 9 7 6 3
♦ A K 8 7 6 5 4                ♦ 2
♣ 8                            ♣ 9 6 5 3 2

              ♠ K Q J 9 5 3
              ♥ K J 2
              ♦ 10 3
              ♣ Q 4
```

This is an easy hand when you think about it. As long as partner can be counted on to give count when he is expected to, defenses like this one are available. If you can't count on partner to give count, you would have an impossible decision.

West Deals + No One Vulnerable

WEST	NORTH	EAST	SOUTH
1♠	Dbl	2♠	4♥
All pass			

NORTH
- ♠ J 7
- ♥ K 6 4 2
- ♦ A Q 8 3
- ♣ K 10 4

WEST
- ♠ A K 8 6 4
- ♥ A 8 7
- ♦ 9
- ♣ J 9 7 5

YOU LEAD THE ♠A and East plays the nine. Is East saying he likes spades or is it a suit preference for diamonds? What is your plan?

In defense, there are three messages you can give your partner.

1. You can give an attitude signal saying you like or dislike what he is doing.
2. You can give a count signal telling him how many cards you have in a particular suit.
3. You can give a suit preference signal telling him indirectly which suit you would like him to shift to.

Here is a useful rule which should help you sort out what is going on.

RULE: A suit preference signal takes a back seat to both of the other signals.

If a signal can be interpreted as attitude, it is so interpreted.

If a signal can be interpreted as count, it is so interpreted.

A suit preference signal is always the last interpretation. Don't fall in love with suit preference signals. Doing so will quickly corrupt your defense. Partner's ♠9 is therefore encouraging, showing the queen. Remember the bidding? Partner raised spades. He is not showing a doubleton.

Should you cash the ♠K or should you lead to partner's queen?

Neither. Partner is telling you he has the ♠Q. What you do with this information is up to you. On this hand you can use this information. Switch to the ♦9. Your plan is to get in with the ♥A and then to lead to partner's ♠Q. He will give you a diamond ruff and that will be down one.

```
              ♠  J 7
              ♥  K 6 4 2
              ♦  A Q 8 3
              ♣  K 10 4

♠  A K 8 6 4                    ♠  Q 9 5 3
♥  A 8 7                        ♥  9 5
♦  9                            ♦  J 4 2
♣  J 9 7 5                      ♣  Q 8 6 3

              ♠  10 2
              ♥  Q J 10 3
              ♦  K 10 7 6 5
              ♣  A 2
```

The winning defense, once you think of it, it isn't too hard to find.

The key is not to lose track of the bidding. If you remember that partner raised spades, you will realize that the ♠9 can't be a doubleton. It can only be an encouraging card telling you he has the queen.

QUICKIE

When on lead against a suit contract, you should almost never lead an ace and you should never underlead an ace. Even if partner overcalled in a suit along the way, you should not rush to lead the ace of partner's suit. If you have a doubleton ace in partner's suit it is reasonable to lead the suit, but you should still look for another lead first.

West Deals + No One Vulnerable

WEST	NORTH	EAST	SOUTH
1♠	Pass	Pass	2♥
2♠	4♥	All pass	

NORTH
♠ 10 5 4 2
♥ A 6 5
♦ K Q
♣ A J 10 5

EAST
♠ 8 3
♥ 9 3
♦ 10 8 6 5 4 3
♣ 6 3 2

WEST LEADS THE ♠A and king. A little surprisingly, South follows both times with the seven and nine. West now leads the ♠6 and dummy plays the five. What's going on? Doesn't partner have the queen and jack? He did open the bidding and he did rebid them. What's up?

West has to have five spades so it's clear he is underleading the ♠QJ when he could just as well have led the queen. Since he could have led the queen, it's clear he wants you to ruff this spade lead. That may mean he is looking for a trump promotion. The ♥9 isn't that big a trump, but it is the best you have. Play it and hope partner is doing the right thing.

♠	10 5 4 2	
♥	A 6 5	
♦	K Q	
♣	A J 10 5	

♠ A K Q J 6	♠ 8 3
♥ K 10 7	♥ 9 3
♦ 9 7 2	♦ 10 8 6 5 4 3
♣ K 7	♣ 6 3 2

♠	9 7
♥	Q J 8 4 2
♦	A J
♣	Q 9 8 4

West has defended well. By leading the ♠6, he woke East up to the necessity of ruffing. Had West led the queen, East would not have thought of ruffing. The effect of this defense is that declarer has to overruff with the ♥J. West now has the heart spots to ensure two heart tricks. Without the uppercut West would have gotten just one trump trick.

Note South's aggressive 2♥ balancing bid. It's reasonable. As you saw, it got his side to a good game that went down because of the good defense.

East Deals + North-South Vulnerable

WEST	NORTH	EAST	SOUTH
		Pass	Pass
4♦	Dbl	5♦	5♠
Pass	6♠	All pass	

NORTH
♠ A Q 10 7
♥ A Q 10 4
♦ 8
♣ A K J 9

EAST
♠ J
♥ 9 8 7 3
♦ A 3
♣ Q 10 6 5 4 2

AFTER A HECTIC auction that included a daring 5♦ bid from East, West leads the ♦2 against 6♠. You win the ace and declarer drops the ten. What do you do now? Are you sure or are you guessing?

The correct play is clear. It is not a guess.

West is ruffing clubs and you should know it. How do you know? You know because of partner's lead. West opened the bidding with 4♦. Whatever else West has, he has a fistful of diamonds. What, therefore, is the ♦2? Is it fourth best? Impossible.

Terence Reese put a name to this lead. He called it an 'alarm clock' lead. The rule is this. If partner leads a card that makes no sense at all, consider what it might be. Here, it is a suit preference signal saying he wants to ruff a club. You come to this conclusion because it can't be accounted for any other way. All reasonable interpretations are impossible. By default, the only thing left is suit preference.

```
                    ♠  A Q 10 7
                    ♥  A Q 10 4
                    ♦  8
                    ♣  A K J 9

    ♠  8 5                          ♠  J
    ♥  J 5 2                        ♥  9 8 7 3
    ♦  K Q J 9 7 6 5 2              ♦  A 3
    ♣  −                            ♣  Q 10 6 5 4 2

                    ♠  K 9 6 4 3 2
                    ♥  K 6
                    ♦  10 4
                    ♣  8 7 3
```

Give West credit for a good lead. If West had led a reflex ♦K, East might or might not do the right thing, but he would have had to think twice about it. East would have to overtake the king, and then talk himself into leading a club. West's thoughtful lead did two things. It forced East to take the ace and it woke East up (alarm clock!) to the fact that something was going on.

POSTMORTEM

After observing the winning defense, take a second off to look at the bidding. All the bids were sane and the final contract was excellent. It pays off to two doses of bad luck. First, West is ruffing clubs. Second, the defenders found a way to get that ruff.

East Deals + No One Vulnerable

WEST	NORTH	EAST	SOUTH
		Pass	1NT*
Pass	3NT	All pass	

*15–17

NORTH
♠ 10 7 2
♥ A K 10
♦ Q J 8 7 6
♣ Q 9

EAST
♠ A 6 4
♥ 8 7 6 4 3
♦ 9 5
♣ 10 3 2

WEST LEADS THE ♣5 and dummy wins with the queen. You discourage with the two.

At trick two, declarer finesses the ♦Q to West's king. West leads the ♠3 and you take your ace. What now?

The ♣10?

Other?

Return the ♠6. West led a little spade, which shows interest in spades. If West wanted you to return a club, he would have led a high spade spot-card to tell you he has no interest in spades.

It is important to have the understanding that when you shift to a little card in a new suit you are showing interest in the new suit and when you shift to a big spot card in a new suit, you do not like the new suit. How else can you tell partner what you want him to do?

Note that you should return the ♠6. If you had started with the ♠A654, you would return the four. You are trying to tell partner how many spades you have. If you started with four or more cards in the suit partner leads, you return your original fourth best. With three only, you return the higher card. Hopefully, partner can read it. Here's the layout:

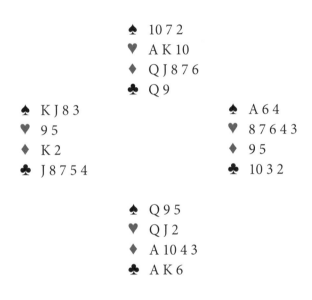

```
                  ♠  10 7 2
                  ♥  A K 10
                  ♦  Q J 8 7 6
                  ♣  Q 9
   ♠  K J 8 3                    ♠  A 6 4
   ♥  9 5                        ♥  8 7 6 4 3
   ♦  K 2                        ♦  9 5
   ♣  J 8 7 5 4                  ♣  10 3 2
                  ♠  Q 9 5
                  ♥  Q J 2
                  ♦  A 10 4 3
                  ♣  A K 6
```

If East-West don't have this agreement, East might return a club, allowing declarer to take his ten tricks.

POSTMORTEM

This is a frequently recurring theme. Remember the above rule. If you want partner to return your new suit, lead a little card. If you want him to return your original suit, lead a high card. It would be a shame to have partner return the wrong suit.

East Deals + North-South Vulnerable

WEST	NORTH	EAST	SOUTH
		Pass	Pass
3♣	Dbl	4♣	4♠
All pass			

NORTH
- ♠ A J 7 3
- ♥ K Q 9 6 4
- ♦ K Q 3
- ♣ 8

EAST
- ♠ K 2
- ♥ A 10 3 2
- ♦ 8 7 2
- ♣ 10 6 4 3

WEST LEADS THE ♥5 to your ace. South follows with the jack. What do you think is happening? Did partner lead a singleton heart? Or was partner just making a neutral lead? What is your plan?

The ♥5 is surely a singleton.

Declarer has made a falsecard, attempting to throw you off the track. Consider the alternatives. If that isn't a singleton heart, it has to be from the ♥875, these being the missing hearts. Would West really lead a heart from this holding? Hard to believe that that would be his best lead.

You should play partner for a singleton heart for two reasons. Firstly, it doesn't make sense for partner to lead a heart if it isn't a singleton. Secondly, if partner has a singleton heart, it will be easy to set 4♠ if partner has either minor-suit ace to cash. Just return a heart and give partner a ruff.

Is that all there is to this hand?

No.

You must be careful. If you carelessly return the ♥2 or ♥3, West may decide you have a club entry. Remember, you did raise clubs. Your partner doesn't know you have the ♠K and he might underlead the ♣A hoping for a second heart ruff. Partner will be entitled to do this because he will read a small heart as suit preference for clubs. Don't embarrass partner. Return the ♥10 for him to ruff.

♠	A J 7 3	
♥	K Q 9 6 4	
♦	K Q 3	
♣	8	

♠ 9 6		♠ K 2
♥ 5		♥ A 10 3 2
♦ 10 6 5 4		♦ 8 7 2
♣ A Q J 9 5 2		♣ 10 6 4 3

♠	Q 10 8 5 4
♥	J 8 7
♦	A J 9
♣	K 7

Look at this hand from West's point of view. West can see a way to beat 4♠ if East has the ♣K, which is likely given East's club raise. But, if East returns the ♥10, that is clearly a suit preference for diamonds.

West will cash the ♣A and will lead a diamond to East's 'ace'. East doesn't have it, but when he takes the setting trick with the ♠K, West will probably forgive him.

Taking care of partner

This is known as taking care of partner. He will appreciate it.

Note West's third-seat 3♣ bid. An excellent tactic in third seat. Give West credit for enterprise. Note also that South bid 4♠. South doesn't really have a 4♠ bid but he has too much to pass. 4♠ would have made without the heart ruff so it was a sane contract.

QUICKIE

Consider all the bidding when you are making your opening lead. Especially, don't forget the passes. If your partner didn't double a Stayman 2♣ bid, or a 5♦ response to Blackwood, or a 4♥ cuebid, you have a mild reason to look beyond these suits for your opening lead.

West Deals + No One Vulnerable

WEST	NORTH	EAST	SOUTH
2♠	3♥	Pass	3NT
All pass			

NORTH
♠ 9 5 4
♥ K Q J 9 8 7
♦ J
♣ K Q J

EAST
♠ A 3
♥ 10 5 3
♦ 6 4 3
♣ A 8 6 5 3

WEST LEADS THE ♠Q. You take your ace and return the three. South wins the king. At trick three declarer leads a club. You win your ace and return...?

You can't answer this question until you ask one of your own. Which question is that?

To know the right return now you need to know which spade partner played at trick two. I will tell you that he played the jack.

Does this help?

West's play of the ♠J is a standard suit preference. It is not an information situation. You already know exactly what partner has in spades. His ♠J is trying to tell you that his entry is in hearts. It looks strange to return a heart but partner told you to. Listen to him.

```
                    ♠  9 5 4
                    ♥  K Q J 9 8 7
                    ♦  J
                    ♣  K Q J

♠  Q J 10 8 7 6                          ♠  A 3
♥  A 4 2                                 ♥  10 5 3
♦  9 8                                   ♦  6 4 3
♣  4 2                                   ♣  A 8 6 5 3

                    ♠  K 2
                    ♥  6
                    ♦  A K Q 10 7 5 2
                    ♣  10 9 7
```

I have said that suit preference takes a secondary role in defence to other signals.

They are an important part of good defense, though, as long as they are used without confusion. There are two or three common situations. This is one of them. West wants to tell East that he has a heart entry. As you can see, West has to get the message across right away. West doesn't have time to waste. This is an unusual hand in that declarer has a hidden seven-card suit. Normally, East could return a diamond or even a club and survive. But not this time. Better to have your signals in order.

South Deals + No One Vulnerable

THE THEME FOR this hand (and the next two) reflects one of the most important moments for a defender. I will show you all four hands so you can easily see what's happening.

         ♠ K 4 2
         ♥ K Q 7 4
         ♦ 9 3 2
         ♣ 5 4 3

♠ 8 7 3   ♠ 6 5
♥ A 10 6   ♥ J 9 8 3 2
♦ K 10 6   ♦ A Q 8 4
♣ A 10 8 2   ♣ J 6

         ♠ A Q J 10 9
         ♥ 5
         ♦ J 7 5
         ♣ K Q 9 7

WEST	NORTH	EAST	SOUTH
			1♠
Pass	2♠	All pass	

SOUTH PLAYS IN a comfortable-looking 2♠ contract. West chooses a trump lead, won by South. South immediately leads his singleton heart. Good play by South. West decides to take it. He continues trumps but South has eight winners.

He has:

- Five spade tricks
- Two heart tricks
- One club trick

That's eight tricks.

POSTMORTEM

What's the big deal here? See the next hand.

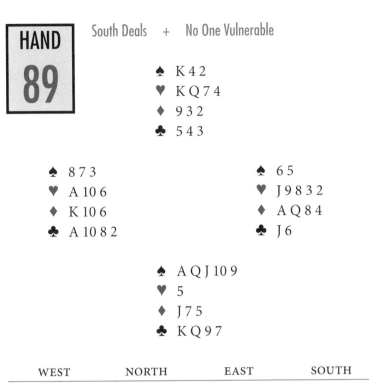

```
                        ♠ K 4 2
                        ♥ K Q 7 4
                        ♦ 9 3 2
                        ♣ 5 4 3

      ♠ 8 7 3                          ♠ 6 5
      ♥ A 10 6                         ♥ J 9 8 3 2
      ♦ K 10 6                         ♦ A Q 8 4
      ♣ A 10 8 2                       ♣ J 6

                        ♠ A Q J 10 9
                        ♥ 5
                        ♦ J 7 5
                        ♣ K Q 9 7
```

WEST	NORTH	EAST	SOUTH
			1♠
Pass	2♠	All pass	

THIS HAND SHOULD look familiar. It's the same as the previous hand. South was in 2♠ and West led a trump. Declarer led a heart and the defense won it. South managed to take eight tricks.

This time, when South leads his heart, West plays low. The ♥K wins.

The play can take various turns from here. Say South plays to his ♣K. West wins and leads another trump. South takes it in his hand and plays the ♣Q and leads a third club, won by West. West leads his third trump.

South wins:

Five spades
One heart
One club

Down one.

The theme here is that when declarer leads toward a holding like KQx in dummy, it is often best for a defender to let declarer have the trick.

POSTMORTEM

The trick is in knowing when to take your ace and when to duck it. If it is the setting trick, it's usually best to take it. Here's the best guideline I can offer:

If you see that declarer does not have lots of potential losers, it could be best to take your ace. If you see he has losers all over the place, as in the hand above, then ducking your ace can be best.

Just be aware that the consequences of taking or not taking the trick can be very important.

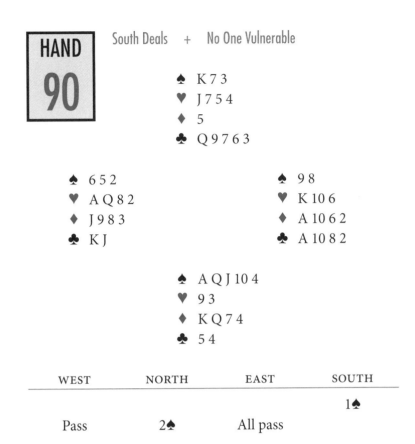

South Deals + No One Vulnerable

♠ K 7 3
♥ J 7 5 4
♦ 5
♣ Q 9 7 6 3

♠ 6 5 2
♥ A Q 8 2
♦ J 9 8 3
♣ K J

♠ 9 8
♥ K 10 6
♦ A 10 6 2
♣ A 10 8 2

♠ A Q J 10 4
♥ 9 3
♦ K Q 7 4
♣ 5 4

WEST	NORTH	EAST	SOUTH
			1♠
Pass	2♠	All pass	

THIS HAND PROVIDES a twist on the problem of the last two hands. South plays in 2♠ with the lead of the ♣6. Declarer wins the trick in dummy and leads the singleton diamond.

The majority of defenders grab their ace and continue leading trumps. Simply stated, East's play turns out to be a losing play. Declarer now has five spades, two diamonds, and a diamond ruff in dummy. Eight tricks.

This layout is essentially the same one you saw on the two previous hands. The difference is that in this layout, the defense sees that a singleton is being led toward the closed hand.

If East takes his ♦A, 2♠ will make. If East plays low, the defense will succeed.

POSTMORTEM

This is a situation that you will see on a daily basis. When declarer leads a singleton from dummy, it is not automatic to jump in with an ace. If declarer has something like KJ2, he will be pleased to see your ace.

I'm hoping that the last three hands will help you realize that the reflex play of taking your ace should not be automatic. My estimate is that not taking your ace will be right much of the time.

QUICKIE

If you are the more experienced player in the partnership, do not insist on using all of your favorite conventions. Your partner won't be able to add five or six ideas all at once. Start with conventions that partner likes and add to them one at a time.

Good as your system may be, your partner won't be comfortable adding Drury, inverted minors, splinter bids, the Jacoby 2NT response to a major, and support doubles en masse. Considering that each of these conventions requires a page of follow-up bids, your partner will be confused for a long time. Keep partner happy.

West Deals   +   No One Vulnerable

WEST	NORTH	EAST	SOUTH
1♦	Pass	Pass	2♣
Pass	Pass	2♦	Pass
Pass	3♣	All pass	

NORTH
♠ K J 3 2
♥ Q 7 6
♦ Q 7 2
♣ Q 8 6

EAST
♠ Q 9 8 5
♥ 9 3
♦ K 9 5 3
♣ 7 4 3

SITTING EAST, YOU pass on the first round. (Would you have responded with the East hand?) South reopens with 2♣, passed to East, who nudges with 2♦. North, in turn, belatedly raises to 3♣, and that is the end of the bidding. A slow motion kind of sequence.

West leads the ♥A (ace from AK) and you show you like this choice by playing the nine. West continues with the ♥K and leads the ten for you to ruff. You have the first three tricks. Where are the next two coming from?

Here is the complete hand:

```
              ♠ K J 3 2
              ♥ Q 7 6
              ♦ Q 7 2
              ♣ Q 8 6

♠ A 7 4                      ♠ Q 9 8 5
♥ A K 10 8                   ♥ 9 3
♦ J 10 8 6                   ♦ K 9 5 3
♣ 10 2                       ♣ 7 4 3

              ♠ 10 6
              ♥ J 5 4 2
              ♦ A 4
              ♣ A K J 9 5
```

Did you lead a diamond back? If you did, declarer had no choice but to finesse it to the queen. When the queen wins, South knows perfectly well where the ♠A is, and he will guess that suit at the end. Making 3♣.

If you return a spade, West wins and and switches to the ♦J. South covers with the queen and you cover with the king. South can concede for down one, but most declarers will try to make 3♣ by finessing the ♠J. Surprise! You have the ♠Q and your diamond return gets your side one more trick. Down two.

The key? When West led the ♥10 for a ruff, he was giving a suit preference signal that he liked the higher ranking suit, spades. Looking at his hand you can see why West didn't want a diamond lead.

POSTMORTEM

West knew what was best for the defense. But if East doesn't listen, it does not matter. Did you listen?

Note North's hand. He has ten points. They're poor points, however. North showed good judgment by staying out of the auction until the very end.

Poor South. He made a reasonable play and paid a price for it.

QUICKIE

Against notrump, when you have the KQ109 of a suit, it is useful to lead the queen rather than the king. If partner has the jack, he will play it and you will know instantly what is going on in this suit. If you lead the king, your partner won't play the jack. If you can't tell where the jack is, you won't be sure how to continue the defense. It's good to have an agreement on this in advance.

HAND

92

South Deals + No One Vulnerable

WEST	NORTH	EAST	SOUTH
			1♣
Pass	1♥	Pass	1♠
Pass	3♠	Pass	4♠
All pass			

WEST
- ♠ J 6 2
- ♥ 8 7 6 5 4
- ♦ K Q 9 4
- ♣ 2

YOU ARE ON lead against South's 4♠. Sometimes you have no good lead, but this time, there are two nice choices. You can lead the singleton club or the ♦K. Assuming you look no further than these two choices, how do you feel about them? Is it a close decision or does one of the leads stand out?

I suggest that in the long run, one of the leads is very good and the other is fairly poor. What is your opinion, and why?

```
              ♠ Q 10 7 5
              ♥ A Q J 2
              ♦ 8 6 3
              ♣ Q 7

♠ J 6 2                          ♠ 8 3
♥ 8 7 6 5 4                      ♥ K 10
♦ K Q 9 4                        ♦ A 10 5
♣ 2                             ♣ J 9 8 5 4 3

              ♠ A K 9 4
              ♥ 9 3
              ♦ J 7 2
              ♣ A K 10 6
```

Opening leads are tough. You can follow the best guidelines and fail miserably. No matter how hard you try, you will get off to some vile opening leads. Take singletons. A singleton lead can be devastating. But if doesn't work, it can be a disaster. Here is a guideline you can put some trust in.

Do not lead a singleton when declarer has bid the suit or has raised his partner. On this hand, you have a nice alternative. The ♦K is sure to set up a trick for you so it has lots going for it. Look at the hand diagram. I admit that the hand is here by my choice, but I promise you that it is a fair example of what I am talking about. If West leads a diamond, the defenders will take the first three diamond tricks and a later heart trick. If West leads a club, declarer will make 4♠ and may end up with an overtrick.

I find that in general, leading a sound honor sequence is better than leading a singleton. If that singleton has been bid by the player on my right, I am less attracted to it than normal.

South Deals + No One Vulnerable

WEST	NORTH	EAST	SOUTH
			1♠
Pass	2♥	Pass	3♥
Pass	3♠	Pass	4♠
All pass			

WEST

♠ 6 4 3
♥ A 10 6 4
♦ A Q 7 5 3
♣ 4

LEADING SINGLETONS IS a popular pastime. Should you lead one here?

One of the qualities a good player has is that he listens to the bidding. It won't help you if you 'know' how the bidding went unless you also know what the bids meant. With that hint, do you think West should lead the ♣4?

♠ K Q 8
♥ K J 8 5 3
♦ 9 2
♣ K 10 8

♠ 6 4 3
♥ A 10 6 4
♦ A Q 7 5 3
♣ 4

♠ 7 2
♥ 2
♦ J 10 8 4
♣ Q J 7 6 5 2

♠ A J 10 9 5
♥ Q 9 7
♦ K 6
♣ A 9 3

If West was paying attention to the bidding, he won't lead clubs.

Go back and review the bidding. It sounds like North has five hearts and South has three. If so, your partner has one. Secondly, your good hand tells you that your partner has very few high-card points. If you lead the club, your partner won't have an entry to make the lead worthwhile. It's more likely that your partner has a stiff heart and you can give him a ruff. Lead the ♥A. What next?

Be careful. Lead the ♥10, which East will ruff. The reason you led the ten was that you wanted to tell East to return a diamond, not a club. West will win two diamond tricks and will give East a second heart ruff. Down two. Not bad. Had West led a club, declarer would get ten or eleven tricks. Quite a swing.

Do not lose track of the bidding or the play and especially, do not lose track of what these things mean.

South Deals   +   No One Vulnerable

WEST	NORTH	EAST	SOUTH
			1♦
Pass	1♥	Pass	1NT
Pass	3NT	All pass	

NORTH
♠ A K Q
♥ 10 8 4 3
♦ Q J 9
♣ 8 7 3

WEST
♠ 7 5 3
♥ A Q 2
♦ K 7
♣ J 10 9 5 4

COUNT. AT ALL times. When you are declarer, you know all of your side's assets. When you are defending, you see what you have and you have to guess what partner has. Throw in the fact that declarer is trying to fool you and defense becomes a challenging package. Sometimes, you can sort it out.

In this hand, you led the ♣J. East played the two and declarer won with the king. Declarer goes over to the ♠A and leads the ♦Q. East and South play low. You win with your king. What do you do?

Have you been counting? If you were watching, you will recall that East played the ♣2. The evidence is that South has the ♣AKQ and the ♦A. That's thirteen points. Since South's maximum is fourteen points, you know your partner has the ♥K. Play the ♥A and queen and two. The layout:

```
                  ♠  A K Q
                  ♥  10 8 4 3
                  ♦  Q J 9
                  ♣  8 7 3

   ♠  7 5 3                        ♠  J 9 6 4
   ♥  A Q 2                        ♥  K 9 7 5
   ♦  K 7                          ♦  6 3 2
   ♣  J 10 9 5 4                   ♣  6 2

                  ♠  10 8 2
                  ♥  J 6
                  ♦  A 10 8 5 4
                  ♣  A K Q
```

Defending this way is wise only if you have counted the high cards. Having done so, this defense is easier. Care to guess how many players made an overtrick in 3NT when this hand was played?

POSTMORTEM

I suggested South has the ♣AKQ. Why can't your partner have the queen? If he had three to the queen, he would play a higher spot card than the two. If he had the ♣Q2, he would have unblocked his queen. You are entitled to play declarer for the three top club honors.

South Deals   +   No One Vulnerable

WEST	NORTH	EAST	SOUTH
			1NT
Pass	3NT	All pass	

NORTH
- ♠ 8 4 3
- ♥ K J 3
- ♦ A Q 8 7 6
- ♣ J 8

WEST
- ♠ K Q J 10
- ♥ 8 7 5 2
- ♦ 4
- ♣ 7 5 4 2

WEST LED THE ♠K and East signaled with the nine. West continued with the queen and East played the two. West played a third round, putting East in with the ace. South followed to all three spades. Three spade tricks for East-West, not four. Who goofed?

This is the hand that led to the defensive disaster:

```
              ♠ 8 4 3
              ♥ K J 3
              ♦ A Q 8 7 6
              ♣ J 8

♠ K Q J 10                    ♠ A 9 2
♥ 8 7 5 2                     ♥ 10 9 4
♦ 4                           ♦ K 5 3 2
♣ 7 5 4 2                     ♣ 9 6 3

              ♠ 7 6 5
              ♥ A Q 6
              ♦ J 10 9
              ♣ A K Q 10
```

One would think that when you have the KQJ10 and partner has the A92 of a suit and you are on lead against notrump, that your side could manage to take four tricks. Who do you think made the mistake in this hand?

It is agreed that West should lead the ♠K and East should signal with the nine. The error came on the second trick. When West led the queen, he was painting an incorrect picture for East. East thought that West had found an inspired lead from the ♠KQx. From East's point of view, West would play the queen on the second round. If West started with the ♠KQx, it would be an error for East to play the ace.

The fault for the accident is entirely West's. West should lead the ten on the second round. East will know for sure that West does not have ♠KQx and will overtake with the ace. The spade return gets the defenders four tricks now and a diamond later.

Are you sure your partnership would get this one right? Would you get it right if West had the ♠KQ7 and East the ♠A92?

The defensive problem shown above comes in various guises. Here are a few of them. In all cases, the bidding is 1NT–3NT. West is on lead with these spade holdings.

♠ 7 5 2

♠ Q J 10 9 8

Your queen wins the trick. Partner plays the six and declarer plays the three. The correct play is to continue with the ten. This promises the jack so East knows to unblock his king.

♠ 7 5 2

♠ Q J 10 9 8   ♠ K 6 4

♠ A 3

East has to do that else the spade suit will be blocked.

Here's another layout to consider. For whatever reason, you have chosen to lead the ♠Q from a three-card holding in hope of finding partner's suit. It's not an uncommon theme.

♠ 7 5 2

♠ Q J 8

West leads the queen and East plays the nine. He likes your lead.

This time you continue with the jack. The difference is that you are hoping your partner has length in the suit. When you lead the jack, your partner will know your suit isn't headed by the QJ10. He won't unblock his king when he has three of them. Here's the layout. Your lead wasn't as good as you had hoped.

$$\spadesuit \ 7\ 5\ 2$$

$$\spadesuit \ Q\ J\ 8 \qquad\qquad \spadesuit \ K\ 9\ 3$$

$$\spadesuit \ A\ 10\ 6\ 4$$

In this layout, East knows to keep his king. If you are leading as I am suggesting, East will do that. In this way, you will avoid the ultimate disaster of giving declarer three spade tricks.

South Deals   +   No One Vulnerable

WEST	NORTH	EAST	SOUTH
			1NT
Pass	3NT	All pass	

NORTH
- ♠ Q J 10
- ♥ 8 7 2
- ♦ A K Q 8
- ♣ 9 8 3

WEST
- ♠ K 9 7 4 2
- ♥ K 6
- ♦ 6 5 2
- ♣ A 10 6

AGAINST A ROUTINE 1NT–3NT auction, West leads his fourth best spade. Dummy wins with the queen and immediately finesses the ♥Q. West takes it and mulls over his chances. What should West be thinking now?

West should be reflecting on the spade that East played at trick one. In fact, East played the three. Does this help West or is the defense still in a quandary?

```
            ♠ Q J 10
            ♥ 8 7 2
            ♦ A K Q 8
            ♣ 9 8 3

♠ K 9 7 4 2                    ♠ 6 5 3
♥ K 6                          ♥ 10 9 5 4 3
♦ 6 5 2                        ♦ 4 3
♣ A 10 6                       ♣ J 7 5

            ♠ A 8
            ♥ A Q J
            ♦ J 10 9 7
            ♣ K Q 4 2
```

Good defenders do more than just take tricks. If you're going to do well on defense, you must know what to do with your high cards but you must also know what to do with little ones. If you get dealt a one- or two-point hand, consider this. Your partner is likely to have a pretty good one. If so, he will know you don't have much, but he doesn't know your distribution. Unless you tell him.

Here, West leads the ♣4 to dummy's queen. East has no honor in the suit, but the information he has to give is just as important. East's play of the ♠3 is not a discouraging card. It's an effort to tell West how many spades East has. If East had the ♠53, he would play the five, trying to tell West that he has two of them. East can't have an honor, else he would play it. In such circumstances, you should try to tell partner 'how many'. On this hand, if West knows East has three spades he can lead a second spade, which will drop South's ace. When West gets in with a club, he will have the setting tricks to take.

East's ♠3 might indeed be a singleton. If so, West's spade continuation won't work. But if that's the case, 3NT isn't going down. West's only hope, a reasonable one, is to play a second spade, which works if South has two. The big deal here is that East is able to communicate useful information at trick one.

When you are defending a hand, you and your partner will be signaling information to each other. If you are on the same wavelength, you and partner will receive the messages and will interpret them as intended. Good defense requires this.

If you play a high spade to tell partner you like spades and partner interprets it as a suit preference for hearts, the result will usually be bad.

One thing you must avoid is giving partner bad information. If you decide to fool declarer with some unusual play, remember that partner is also looking at your cards and he is likely to make an error on your behalf.

Here's a true story from eons ago. I was playing bridge with a good player who had a kibitzer of interest to him. Declarer was running off some winners. At one point, I saw that I was going to have to discard two hearts from a holding of J98. I hated hearts and did not want partner to lead them. I did what I had to do. I discarded the ♥8. On the next trick, I discarded the nine. I was happy that I had been able to make two discards because my eight, then nine, was clearly a discouraging signal. What happened? Partner got in and immediately led a heart. We got a terrible result. My partner asked why I played the nine. I showed that I had played the eight before playing the nine. The kibitzer said it all. "I guess you have to pay attention to all the cards."